The Quotable Fulton Sheen

Edited by GEORGE J. MARLIN,
RICHARD P. RABATIN,
and JOHN L. SWAN

*With a Foreword
by John Cardinal O'Connor*

The Quotable Fulton Sheen

A Topical Compilation
of the Wit, Wisdom, and Satire
of Archbishop Fulton J. Sheen

AN IMAGE BOOK
DOUBLEDAY
New York · London · Toronto · Sydney · Auckland

An Image Book
Published by Doubleday, a division of Bantam Doubleday Dell Publishing
Group, Inc., 666 Fifth Avenue, New York, New York 10103.

IMAGE, DOUBLEDAY, and the portrayal of a cross intersecting a circle are
trademarks of Doubleday, a division of Bantam Doubleday Dell Publishing
Group, Inc.

Grateful acknowledgment is made to the Estate of Fulton J. Sheen and to
Doubleday for the bulk of material in this collection.

Library of Congress Cataloging-in-Publication Data

Sheen, Fulton J. (Fulton John), 1895-1979.
    [Selections. 1989]
    The quotable Fulton Sheen: a topical compilation of the wit,
wisdom, and satire of Fulton J. Sheen/with a foreword by
John Cardinal O'Connor; edited by George J. Marlin,
Richard P. Rabatin, and John L. Swan.—1st Image ed.
        p. cm.
    Bibliography: p.
    1. Sheen, Fulton J. (Fulton John), 1895-1979—Quotations.
2. Catholic Church—Apologetic works.   I. Marlin, George J., 1952–
    II. Rabatin, Richard P., 1950–   III. Swan, John L.   IV. Title.
BX4705.S612A25   1989
081—dc20   89-31967

Our Efforts Are Dedicated to

Barbara D. Marlin
Donna A. Rabatin
Private Robert H. Swan (1923-1944)

Preface

In the spring of 1925, a public examination took place before three hundred people at the University of Louvain in Belgium. Professors traveled from all over Europe to question the candidate for the coveted Agrégé en Philosophie—a type of super doctorate. From early morning until late afternoon, the candidate was grilled. When it was over he was sent back to his room to await the verdict. The knock on his door indicated he had passed. The degree of his success would be measured by the beverage served at dinner: water would indicate a mere pass; wine, a pass with distinction. That night, Fulton J. Sheen, the tenth person in forty years to receive the degree and the first American ever to be so honored, was served champagne—the very highest distinction.

The thesis written for that degree became the first of his seventy books and was entitled *God and Intelligence*. In his introduction the great British journalist G. K. Chesterton wrote, "In this book, as in the modern world generally, the Catholic Church comes forward as the one and only real champion of reason." For the next fifty-four years, Fulton Sheen would employ his great gift of reason in his preaching and writing to expose the heresies of the twentieth century.

Fulton John Sheen was born over his father's hardware store in El Paso, Illinois, on May 8, 1895. An outstanding student, Sheen attended St. Victor's College in Bourbonnais, Illinois, and later, realizing he had a religious vocation, entered St. Paul's Seminary in Minnesota.

Ordained a priest on September 25, 1919, he was not assigned to a parish but was sent to The Catholic University of America to pursue graduate studies. Upon earning his master of arts degree, he traveled to Europe for additional education. After receiving a doctorate of philosophy from the University of Louvain and a doctorate in sacred theology from the Angelicum in Rome, Sheen was offered teaching positions at Oxford and at Columbia University. To his bishop, Sheen sent a letter asking, "Which offer should I accept?" The answer was, "Come home."

Father Sheen was appointed curate of St. Patrick's parish—one of the poorest in the diocese. Expecting to spend his life as a parish priest, Sheen happily involved himself in parish life. It was during this time that he began preaching the Lenten course for which he was to become world famous.

In the summer of 1926, Father Sheen was summoned to the office of his bishop, who informed him, "Three years ago I promised you to Bishop Shahan of The Catholic University as a member of the faculty." Sheen asked, "Why did you not let me go there when I returned from Europe?" "Because of the success you had on the other side, I just wanted to see if you would be obedient. So run along now, you have my blessing."

He was appointed to the School of Theology of The Catholic University of America and assigned to the chair of apologetics. In Sheen's own words,

> I loved teaching. I loved it because it seemed so close to the prolongation of the Divine Word. . . .
>
> I felt a deep moral obligation to students; that is why I spent so many hours in preparation for each class. In an age of social justice one phase that seems neglected is the moral duty of professors to give their students a just return for their tuition. This applies not only to the method of teaching but to the content as well. A teacher who himself does not learn is no teacher. Teaching is one of the noblest vocations on earth, for, in the last analysis, the purpose of all education is the knowledge and love of truth.

Sheen was to teach for twenty-five years. The themes of his courses often developed into books: *Religion Without God* (1928), *Old Errors and New Labels* (1931), *Philosophy of Science* (1934), and *Philosophy of Religion* (1948).

During this period, Sheen's reputation as a preacher and Catholic apologist continued to grow, and invitations to speak and preach throughout the nation poured in. In 1928 he was invited by the Paulist Fathers of New York to give a series of sermons that were broadcast on a popular radio station. In 1930 the American Bishops invited Fulton Sheen to represent the Church on NBC's nationally broadcast show "The Catholic Hour," and he appeared on that show until 1951, when he switched from radio to television.

Many believed Sheen had the ability to become the greatest Catholic philosopher of the twentieth century. However, Sheen's duties at The Catholic University became minimal; he eventually taught only one graduate course a year. The chairman of the philosophy department, Father Ignatius Smith, stated, "I was often criticized for not giving him more work, but I felt he was doing more good on the outside."

Yes, Monsignor Sheen (as he became in 1934) was to accomplish much on the outside. He produced at least one book a year, wrote two weekly newspaper columns, became national director of the Society for the Propagation of the Faith, and edited two magazines. Also, he was instrumental in numerous conversions, including Clare Booth Luce, Henry Ford II, Communists Louis Budenz and Elizabeth Bently, and violinist Fritz Kreisler.

Sheen had the rare ability to take complex philosophical and theological concepts and translate them into language the person on the street could understand. Books he authored (e.g., *Liberty, Equality and Fraternity* [1928], *Freedom Under God* [1940], *Whence Come Wars* [1940], *For God and Country* [1941], *A Declaration of Dependence* [1941], *God and War* [1942], and *Communism and the Conscience of the West* [1948]) contributed immeasurably to educating Americans on the evils of nazism, fascism, and communism. As one rereads the works, one recognizes Sheen as a prophet. In 1938 he wrote, "Pilate and Herod were enemies and became friends over the bleeding Body of Christ, so one day communism and Nazism, which are now enemies, will become friends over the bleeding body of Poland."

In 1951, the now Bishop Sheen appeared on stage at Manhattan's Adelphi Theatre and said to America, "Thank you for allowing me into your home." It was the beginning of his award-winning television show, "Life Is Worth Living." He was the first (and possibly only) religious leader to have a show sponsored by a major corporation. Sheen relates:

> When I began television nationally and on a commercial basis, the approach had to be different. I was no longer talking in the name of the Church and under the sponsorship of its bishops. The new method had to be more ecumenical and directed to Catholics, Protestants, Jews and all men of good will. It was no longer a direct presentation of Christian doctrine but rather a reasoned approach to it beginning with something that was common to the audience. Hence, during those television years, the subjects ranged from communism, to art, to science, to humor, aviation, war, etc. Starting with something that was common to the audience and to me, I would gradually proceed from the known to the unknown or to the moral and Christian philosophy. It was the same method Our Blessed Lord used when He met a prostitute at the well. What was there in common between Divine Purity and this woman who had five husbands and was living with a man who was not her husband? The only common denominator was a love of cold water. Starting with that He led to the subject of the waters of everlasting life.

"Life Is Worth Living" was up against "The Milton Berle Show." Every week America asked, "Shall we watch Uncle Miltie or Uncle Fultie?" Sheen's ratings skyrocketed, and Mr. Television was knocked off the air.

The show, which continued until 1957, had an estimated audience of 30 million. The bishop, whose topics covered various subjects from psychology to Irish humor to Stalin, received eight to ten thousand letters a day. In 1964 Sheen appeared on a weekly show entitled "Quo Vadis America," and in 1966, "The Bishop Sheen Show."

On October 28, 1966, Pope Paul VI appointed Fulton Sheen the bishop of Rochester, New York. As he approached his seventy-fifth year in 1969, Bishop Sheen retired from that post and was named by the Holy Father titular archbishop of Newport, Wales. In his autobiography he wrote:

> When I resigned, I did not "retire." I retreaded. I took on another kind of work. I believe that we spend our last days very much the way that we lived. If we have lived with ease, taking our rest, never exerting ourselves, then we have a long dragging out of our days, like a slow leak. If we live intensely, I believe that somehow or other we can work up until the day God draws the line and says: "Now it is finished."

On September 25, 1979, Archbishop Sheen celebrated the sixtieth anniversary of his priesthood. At a small party, he described to friends the three stages of his life. First, the period of vocation, in which there was the calling from God to be a priest. He was devoted to his priesthood and never for a moment wished he had pursued another career. The second period was that of proclamation, the time when he became renowned preaching the Lord's message. The third period was when his love for Christ intensified and he began to experience unspeakable peace. As he stated, "I considered everything a waste except knowing Christ. Anything that is done or read or spoken or enjoyed or suffered that does not bring me closer to Him makes me ask myself: why all this waste?"

On October 2, 1979, in the sanctuary of St. Patrick's Cathedral in New York, Pope John Paul II embraced Archbishop Sheen and told him, "You have written and spoken well of the Lord Jesus. You are a loyal son of the Church."

On December 9, 1979, Archbishop Fulton Sheen died in the Lord. He was buried beneath the main altar at St. Patrick's Cathedral, from which he had preached for so many years.

Fulton Sheen was a remarkable human being. From the 1930s to his death in 1979, he was revered by most Americans. In editing books totaling over twelve thousand pages, we soon realized Archbishop Sheen's works were a tremendous hard-hitting indictment of dehumanizing, atheistic, pseudointellectual, scientistic, and evil fads—in short, the pathetic ideological edifice for which the twentieth century shall be condemned by future historians. The following passage is exemplary:

There is no one in this country and few in Western Civilization who have not had these false assumptions driven into his mind by the press, by education, by word of mouth, until they became unchallenged dogmas even for those who wanted no dogmas. False prophets a few years ago were saying that progress is natural and inevitable; that evil and sin are just relics of the fall in evolution; that the wars of the past were but the growing pains of civilization and we would soon grow out of their immaturity; that goodness increases with the years, that evil and error decline; that science, which has gained mastery over nature, will soon master the imperfection of man; that, since we have done so much in our time, we will soon do everything; that evolution takes the place of

Providence, science supplants grace; and psychoanalysis eradicates guilt; that the theory of the natural goodness of man enunciated by Rousseau, and which was given a biological kick by Darwin, means that nothing can stop us from getting better and better; that men no longer need God, whom they called a "pious extra," because, our professors told us, God was not a Creator but a creature of man's thinking; that evil, still spoken of by the Catholic Church, is due to ignorance and can be cured by education and improved glands; that the Catholic opposition to divorce as destructive of the family is due to its reactionism and its ignorance of the new social theories; that the Kingdom of God is on earth, and that the primitive man who became civilized man will soon be the superman needing no God, because God is man and man is God; that to be "unmodern" is a greater curse than to be a sinner; . . . that anyone who protests against the fulfillment of history within the domains of space and time is either a Catholic, or an antiprogressive, or both; that freedom means the right to do whatever you please; and that to inculcate in the growing child a sense of right and wrong is to be unprogressive (what modern man could live under the stigma of being called "unprogressive"? The shades of John Dewey would haunt him all his waking nights!); . . . that universal education can root out the propensity to evil; that history is an uninterrupted progress at the beginning of which were millions of evils, then later only half a million, and in the very near future, according to the major prophet H. G. Wells, there will be *A Brave, New World*.

We are grateful to all those who kindly helped us in our efforts, but any inaccuracies herein must rest on the shoulders of the editors. Special thanks to Larry and Pat Azar, Joseph Bierbauer, Ronald Carolonza, Msgr. Eugene V. Clark, Ph.D., Michael G. Crofton, John P. DeMaio, Alan and Chris Jones, Kenneth McAlley, Joe Mysak, Rev. George William Rutler, S.T.D., Thomas Walsh, and Charles G. Woram.

Finally, our gratitude to Archbishop Sheen's "Lovely Lady Dressed in Blue"—the Mother of Christ, whose Divine Son alone makes "Life Worth Living."

GEORGE J. MARLIN
RICHARD P. RABATIN
JOHN L. SWAN
New York City
February 1989

Foreword

No one could have grown up truly Catholic in the thirties whose father didn't have him listen to Monsignor Fulton J. Sheen every Sunday afternoon on "The Catholic Hour." It was easy listening. I never had to be forced. On the contrary, those Sunday afternoons gave me my lifelong passion for good preaching.

I wasn't thrilled merely by the sterling silver of the famous Sheen voice, however, or intrigued by his lifelong retention of an Oxford accent, or hypnotized by his magical turning of a phrase. The man had something to say.

When a world was bemused by communism, he unmasked communism. When the world was beguiled by fascism, he unmasked fascism. When the same world was befuddled by nazism, he unmasked nazism. I will never forget his Sunday afternoon declamation, "Red shirts, brown shirts, black shirts are all the same." That was so much of his gift—to see relationships that others missed. Hence, he could say of the swastika that it had started out to be a cross but had double-crossed itself.

He saw extraordinary relationships among Gospel figures unseen by others. He offered insights into Gospel events that opened new horizons for prayer. His lifelong romance with the Mother of God made him her personal bard, her happy troubadour. Whenever he recited "Lovely Lady Dressed in Blue," Mary won countless new and devoted sons and daughters.

A book of Sheen selections is a fine idea indeed, because he wrote the way he talked, in unhackneyed aphorisms, easily remembered for chewing upon during working hours or while at prayer or when tempted to discouragement. The heaviest of them is light in spirit, designed to lift hearts and minds.

I was there the day the Pope hugged Archbishop Sheen. In October of 1979 I had been a bishop all of six months, but it was long enough to get me in to St. Patrick's Cathedral when Pope John Paul II, still a new pope, entered the sanctuary and saw the old archbishop. The embrace flooded the cathedral with tears. The Holy Father's words flooded Archbishop Sheen's heart with joy. The archbishop said the Pope told him, in essence, "You have written and spoken well of the Lord Jesus. You are a loyal son of the Church."

He was that, to the hilt, and it was as a loyal son of the Church that he repeated so frequently the prophetic words I have never forgotten: "What the world needs is a voice that is right not when the world is right, but a voice that is right when the world is wrong."

JOHN CARDINAL O'CONNOR
February 27, 1989

The Quotable Fulton Sheen

A

Absolution

To recommend political and economic panaceas for the world problem of dehumanized forgotten man, is like recommending face powder for jaundice, or an alcohol rub for cancer. It is not our bodies that are ill; the soul of civilization is sick. The world is in a state of mortal sin and it needs absolution.

c., 78

Academia

How many universities in our land founded as religious institutions for the propagation of a particular Christian creed, today adhere to the creeds they were founded to propagate?

w.w., 7–8

Academic Freedom

There is no danger of our universities and colleges losing academic freedom because professors are asked, "Are you a loyal, true American?" But there is grave danger that academic freedom may be lost by teachers saying that the students under them are not free; that they are determined economically, biologically, or socially.

L. I, 234

Adversity

Sin brings adversity and adversity is the expression of God's condemnation of evil, the registering of Divine Judgment.

D.V., 25

Advertisements

Today cars are sold by men on horseback through the medium of television. A woman is seen doing dishes in a mink coat; no woman in a kitchen is ever over thirty; cigarettes are smoked only by boys and girls in love—all these inanities are part of the conspiracy against reason.

O.B., 57

Advertising

Advertising tries to stimulate our sensuous desires, converting luxuries into necessities, but it only intensifies man's inner misery. The business world is bent on creating hungers which its wares never satisfy, and thus it adds to the frustrations and broken minds of our times.

L.H., 74

Age of Reason

The so-called "Age of Reason" was really an Age of Unbelief for its strongest protagonists were corrosive men like Hume, Kant, Voltaire, who measured the growth of reason by its alienation from God. . . . The sovereignty of reasonable people replaced the sovereignty of God.

P.W., 15

The Aged

Modern civilization has little respect for the aged for the same reason it has little for tradition. There is a love for the antique but not for the ancient. Yet the aged are to culture what memory is to the mind.

W.I., 117

Agnosticism

. . . today those who do not have faith do not even know what they disbelieve. Having abandoned all certitudes they have no standards by which to judge even their own agnosticism.

S.V., 54

Agnosticism is not an intellectual position, but a moral position, or better still, an intellectual defense for a life which is afraid of the light.

W.I., 140

Agony in the Garden

Sin is in the blood. It can be read in the face of the libertine, the alcoholic, the criminal and the assassin. The shedding of blood, therefore, represented the emptying of sin. The Agony of the Garden and its bloody sweat were related to our sins which the Lord took upon Himself, for "Christ never knew sin, and God made him into sin for us" (II CORINTHIANS 5:21).

P.N., 4

Alcoholic

There is a vast difference between the individual who gets drunk because he loves liquor and the one who does it because he hates or fears something else so much that he has to run away from it. The first becomes the drunkard, the second the alcoholic. The drunkard pursues the exhilaration of liquor; the alcoholic pursues the obliteration of memory.

L.H., 56

Alcoholism

If alcoholism is a disease for which there is no responsibility, why is it that the victims demand praise for the recovery, but not blame for the indulgence? Preaching to others, they say: "I was once in the gutter. Now look at me." Tuberculosis is a disease, but one never hears of tubercular patients going about parading their recovery from tuberculosis. It is because there is little element of freedom involved in a recovery from tuberculosis or diabetes, but there is some freedom involved in the cure of alcoholism.

L.5, 79

Alone

Say not, then, "religion is a private affair" any more than your birth is a private affair. You cannot be born alone; you cannot live alone; you cannot even die alone for your death is tied up with property or at least with burial. You cannot practise religion alone any more than you can love alone.

P.R., 77

America

Freedom is not just something with which we are born; it is something we achieve. America did not receive a perpetual endowment of freedom; it has had to struggle and fight to preserve it. Freedom is not an heirloom or an antique; it is a life that must fight against the corrosive powers of death and nourish itself on the daily bread of goodness and virtue.

O.B., 164

America's greatest enemy is not from without, but from within, and that enemy is hate: hatred of races, peoples, classes and religions. If America ever dies, it will be not through conquest but suicide.

P.R., 217

American Democracy is founded on the principle of the essential spiritual equality of all men.

P.W., 25

Americans

. . . Americans . . . judge the value of everything by its size.

O.B., 41

Analyst's Prayer

"I thank Thee, O Lord . . . that there is no such thing as guilt, that sin is a myth, and that Thou, O Father, art only a projection of my father complex. There may be something wrong with my repressed instincts, but there is nothing wrong with my soul. I contribute 10 per cent of my income to the Society for the Elimination of Religious Superstitions, and I diet for my figure three times a week. Oh, I thank Thee that I am not like the rest of men, those nasty people, such as the Christian there in the back of the temple who thinks that he is a sinner, that his soul stands in need of grace, that his conscience is burdened with extortion, and that his heart is weighted down with a crime of injustice. I may have an Oedipus complex, but I have no sin."

P.S., 63

Anarchist

It will be seen that many who follow a philosophy of political anarchy have already been committed in their personal lives to a philosophy of animalism.

D.L., 79

Angels

The decline of belief in angels does not prove that the world has gotten wiser, but rather that it has become materialistic. The principle reason why angels have lost their following is because angels are created substances of pure intelligence, but devoid of all bodily qualities and characteristics. The modern mind lives in a closed universe in the sense that man is believed to be just an animal devoid of an immortal soul, and with no other purpose in life than to attain security and enjoy pleasure.

T.T., 16

Anger

Bad temper is an indication of a man's character; every man can be judged by the things which make him mad.

L.A., 115

To the bad conscience God appears always the God of wrath. The boy who broke the vase by throwing a ball at it, says to his mother: "Now Mummy, don't get mad." Anger is not in the mother; anger is in the boy's projection to his mother of his own sense of justice. Anger is not in God; anger is in our disordered selves.

P.R., 50

Animal versus Man

No pig ever had ulcers, and not even the most erotic rooster has had a mother complex.

L.5, 185

Annunciation

What is called the Annunciation was actually God asking the free consent of a creature to help Him to be incorporated into humanity.

L.C., 23

The Antireligious

Those who hate religion are seeking religion; those who wrongly condemn are still seeking justice; those who overthrow order are seeking a new order; even those who blaspheme are adoring their own gods—but still adoring.

R.S., 79

Anti-Semitism

For a Catholic, to be anti-Semitic is to be un-Catholic.

L.A., 124

An anti-Semite seeks to justify his hatred on the ground that the Jews are our enemies. Even if they were, is not a Christian supposed to love his enemies?

L.A., 126

How does the Christian ever expect the Jew to accept the Christian code unless he, the Christian, acts like a Christian? Hating the Jew will do more harm to the Christian soul than it will ever do to the Jew.

L.A., 126

A Jew knows that anti-Semitism is not due to Christianity, because he knows that his people were persecuted before the advent of Christianity.

L.A., 131

Anti-Semitism and Christianity

Christianity cannot be anti-Semitic, because it honors such Jews as Abraham, Isaac, Jacob, Moses, David. Were not the twelve Apostles Jews? Was not the first Pope a Jew? Does not the Church use the Old Testament as much as the Synagogue does? Have not its scholars defended the authenticity of the Old Testament?

L.A., 133

Apostle

The Apostles were the nucleus of the Church, the new Israel, the first visible manifestation of Christ's Mystical Body. That is why on Pentecost they chose one out of the community of 120 to take the place of Judas. The successor had to be an eyewitness of the Gospel events; that was the absolute condition of being an Apostle.

W.L., 44

Appeasement

You cannot oppose an ideology with an opinion, or a philosophy of life with appeasing compromises. The mere fact that you give your right arm to a bear is no guarantee that he will not take your left.

C.P., 98

Aquinas, St. Thomas

His first principle was: You cannot begin religion with faith; there must be a reason for faith and a motive for belief.

L.2, 46

Arguments

The hardest thing to find in the world today is an argument. Because so few are thinking, naturally there are found but few to argue.

O.E., 3

Aristocracy (Modern)

[The] new aristocracy does not care what cause it promotes so long as it can maintain its privileged position.

D.D., 8

Armageddon

The conflict of the future will be between a God-religion and a State religion, between Christ and anti-Christ in political disguise.

C.P., 39

Art

Because of the spiritual power in man, he alone is able to produce art. Art is the projection of the ideal through the real, and man alone is capable of ideals.

L.4, 130

Art and Philosophy

There is no such thing as understanding art in any period apart from the philosophy of that period. Philosophy inspires art, and art reflects philosophy. We can never tell what the art of an age is unless we know what is the thought of the age. If the thought is lofty and spiritual, art will be lofty and spiritual; if the thought is base and material, art will be base and material. If the thought is of the heavens heavenly, art will be of the heavens heavenly; if the thought is of the earth earthly, art will be of the earth earthly.

O.E., 119

Asceticism

The end of all self-discipline is love. Anyone, therefore, who makes the taming of animal impulses the end and prime purpose of his life —as some of the Oriental mystics do—achieves the negation of the flesh but not the affirmation of the spirit. St. Paul told the Corinthians that, if a man should deliver his body to be burned, it would profit him nothing unless he had Divine Love.

P.S., 168

Atheism

Atheism is nihilism; Godlessness is nothingness.

D.L., 178

. . . atheism is the emptiness of idolatry.

F.D., 220

Atheism has moved from the intellectual plane, where it was in the last century, to the existential plane; from the level of proving atheism to the living it; from the nonexistence of God to the existence of humanity. Atheism posits a new god, namely, Man.

G.T., 137

There are two kinds of "atheism": the atheism of the right, which professes to love God and ignores neighbor; and the atheism of the left, which professes to love neighbor and ignores God.

M.P., 69-70

Atheism (Modern)

Today's atheism is not passive, like the old-fashioned atheism, which allowed believers to exist alongside of it; it is now militant, active, political, proselytizing, and communistic.

L.H., 36

Atheism (New)

For the new atheism is not like the old, theoretical atheism, which prided itself on being intellectually compounded of a little science, anthropology, and comparative religion. The new atheism is not of the intellect, but of the will; it is an act of free and eager rejection of morality and its demands. It starts with the affirmation of self and the denial of the moral law.

L.H., 36

Atheist

We do not have to fear atomic bombs; but we do have to fear Godless men.

D.L., 179

The most perverse atheist can love Godlessness only because such an idea seems good.

L.H., 49

The atheist . . . is properly defined as the person who has no invisible means of support.

S.W., 54

Atheist (Modern)

. . . the modern atheist is always angered when he hears anything said about God and religion—he would be incapable of such a resentment if God were only a myth.

P.S., 228

Authoritarianism

Peace is the tranquillity of order—of true order. It is easy to understand why so many minds of this century have flocked to the authoritarianism of the Nazi, the Fascist, or the Communist in their desperation for an ordering principle. Having no true picture of reality, but recognizing the need of *some* guiding principle outside their confused, bewildered, and frustrated minds, they throw themselves into the false ordering of dictatorship.

L.H., 27

Authority

We are witnessing . . . the queer spectacle of a world that began four hundred years ago by hating authority, now falling down before an authority more absolute than history has seen since the advent of Christianity.

C.C., 128

Authoritarianism is based on force, and therefore is physical, but authority is founded on reverence and love, and therefore is moral.

L.5, 245

If it be true that the world has lost its respect for authority, it is only because it lost it first in the home.

O.B., 174

Authority (Church)

There is nothing more misunderstood by the modern mind than the authority of the Church. Just as soon as one mentions the authority of the Vicar of Christ there are visions of slavery, intellectual servitude, mental chains, tyrannical obedience, and blind service on the part of those who, it is said, are forbidden to think for themselves. That is positively untrue. Why has the world been so reluctant to accept the authority of the Father's house? Why has it so often identified the Catholic Church with intellectual slavery?

The answer is, because the world has forgotten the meaning of liberty.

C.C., 128

Avarice

The more people own beyond the limit of things they can personalize and love, the more they will suffer boredom, ennui, and satiety.

O.B., 95

B

Baby

There is something about a baby that disarms, attracts, and makes even the evil want to appear as good.

T.M., 226

Baptism

Now, Bethlehem is the city where the die was struck and Christ Himself is the Die. All the men who have lived and will ever live are the raw material awaiting the stamp of the Divine Original. But in order to be like Him, that is, a sharer of His Divine Life, we must be struck off that die. And the Baptismal font is the new Bethlehem where the copies are made, for there men are re-born again to the Life of God.

P., 10

Beasts

Beasts are divided from man by tears and laughter. Both have to do with the soul rather than the body.

O.B., 44

Beatitudes

The Beatitudes cannot be taken alone: they are not ideals; they are hard facts and realities inseparable from the Cross of Calvary. What He taught was self-crucifixion: to love those who hate us; to pluck out eyes and cut off arms in order to prevent sinning; to be clean on the inside when the passions clamor for satisfaction on the outside; to forgive those who would put us to death; to overcome evil with good; to bless those who curse us; to stop mouthing freedom until we have justice, truth and love of God in our hearts as the condition of freedom; to live in the world and still keep oneself unpolluted from it; to deny ourselves sometimes legitimate pleasures in order the better to crucify our egotism—all this is to sentence the old man in us to death.

L.C., 119

Beauty

Beauty without virtue is like a fair flower that has an offensive odor. But true beauty bathes in that light without which nothing is beautiful. Beauty is a gift of God, like the rain. He allows the rain to fall upon the just and the wicked, and He gives beauty not only to the good, but even to the wicked. Wicked beauty strikes the eye, but the inner beauty of grace wins the soul.

G.T., 54

Beelzebub

The very fact that in World War II we chose to fight in alliance with one form of totalitarianism against the other two forms, though all were intrinsically wicked, proves not only the basic sympathy between Western materialism and communism but also the grave mistake of trying to drive the Devil out with Beelzebub.

C.C., 52

Behaviorism

Man is a machine and the Behaviorists are his prophets. The fad in psychology called Behaviorism has produced something flattering to our machine age. . . . By asserting that man is just a series of twitchings, muscle-squirmings, visceral reactions, and gland-oozings, by stressing the fact that human activities are due to "something going on in the guts and the glands," Behaviorism is supposed to have done away with the necessity of appealing to a soul or a vital principle in man. In a word, the Behaviorists make psychology a study of the psychological reactions of the organism as a whole; they analyze human nature, not with the eighteenth century, into sensations and ideas, but rather into the completely biological reaction of the nervous system to specific stimuli.

O.E., 199

Belief

Nothing shows more thoughtlessness than the idiocy that "it makes no difference what you believe; it all depends on the way you live." On the contrary, we act on our beliefs; our ideas are motor-springs in action; if our thinking is bad our actions will be bad.

D.L., 59

Benefactor

There is much money given away, but little of it is used for the soul. Some give it away in order to have their name glorified on the door of a hospital or a university. Men who have had very little education are conspicuous for endowing libraries, that they might create the impression of being learned, which they are not.

W.H., 152

Bergson, Henri

. . . it is unfortunate that some men who think poorly can write so well. Bergson has written a philosophy grounded on the assumption that the greater comes from the less, but he has so camouflaged that intellectual monstrosity with mellifluous French that he has been credited with being a great and original thinker.

O.E., 6–7

Betrayal

The greatest betrayals come from within.

L.2, 205

Bible

Never once did Our Lord tell these witnesses of His to write. He Himself only wrote once in His Life, and that was on the sand. But He *did* tell them to preach in His Name and to be witnesses to Him to the ends of the earth, until the consummation of time. Hence those who take this or that text out of the Bible to prove something are isolating it from the historical atmosphere in which it arose, and from the word of mouth which passed Christ's truth.

W.L., 45

Bigot

They do not really hate the Church. They hate only what they mistakenly believe to be the Church. If I had heard the same lies about the Church they have heard, and if I had been taught the same historical perversions as they, with my own peculiar character and temperament, I would hate the Church ten times more than they do.

S.W., 70

Bigotry

Hatred comes from want of knowledge, as love comes from knowledge; thus, bigotry is properly related to ignorance.

W.H., 63

Biography

A man's biography is written in terms not so much of what he causes to happen, but rather what happens *to* him and *in* him. The difference between men is not in the adversity which comes to them, but rather how they meet the adversity.

O.B., 51

Biography (Modern)

It used to be that the most popular biographies were the lives of good men for the sake of imitation, rather than scandals for the sake of making ourselves believe we are more virtuous.

W.I., 12

Birth

There never can be a birth without love.

L.C., 22

Birth Control

It has always struck me as strange that we should pardon a wife, on the grounds of "temporary insanity," for limiting her married life by shooting her husband, and at the same time glorify the same wife as a "progressive free-born woman" because she limits her family by stifling an unborn life. All of which goes to prove that we do not need new laws but expansion of the definitions of old ones, and particularly of the law of murder.

O.E., 290

Bitterness

Bitterness is an incentive to self-destruction.

D.L., 113

Blarney versus Boloney

To tell a woman who is forty, "You look like sixteen," is boloney. The blarney way of saying it is "Tell me how old you are, I should like to know at what age women are most beautiful."

L.1, 187

There is a difference between blarney and boloney. Blarney is the varnished truth; boloney is the unvarnished lie. Blarney is flattery laid on so thin you love it; boloney is flattery laid on so thick you hate it.

L.1, 187

The Blessed Mother

I wonder if it is not true that as the world loses veneration for Christ's mother, it loses also its adoration of Christ.

S.W., 44

Boast

The man who has a right to boast does not have to boast.

T.T., 12

Body

He who forgets that the body is the vestment of the immortal soul is destined for boredom.

L.4, 192

In the eyes of God there is nothing to be ashamed of when the soul clothes the body, but there is a great deal to be ashamed of when the body is put before the soul. That is why the body has to be covered and hidden; like a murderer concealing his victim, we try to hide our crime.

L.5, 239

Books

Any book which inspires us to lead a better life is a good book.

D.L., 132

Books are the most wonderful friends in the world. When you meet them and pick them up, they are always ready to give you a few ideas. When you put them down, they never get mad; when you take them up again, they seem to enrich you all the more.

L.2, 60

A Bore

. . . a bore has been described as a man who deprives one of solitude without ever giving company.

T.T., 169

Boredom

Nothing is as fatiguing as boredom.

P.N., 104

Boys

A boy thinks he never could get too much ice cream, but he soon discovers there is just not enough boy.

P.R., 4

Bravery

. . . it must not be thought that bravery is devoid of fear; rather it is control of fear.

S.V., 14

Broad-mindedness

In order that the world might be made safe for so many conflicting points of view, broad-mindedness was cultivated as the most desirable of all virtues. The man who still believed in truth was often called narrow, while he who cared not to distinguish it from error was praised for his breadth.

F.G., 13

Broad-mindedness (Modern)

It has inspired the idea that we should be broad enough to publish our sins to any psychoanalyst living in a glass house, but never so narrow as to tell them to a priest in a confessional box.

M.T., 166

Brotherhood

To believe in the brotherhood of man without the Fatherhood of God would make men a race of bastards.

L.C., 199

Burden

Help someone in distress and you lighten your own burden; the very joy of alleviating the sorrow of another is the lessening of one's own.

O.B., 145

Business

Business is *not* business—business is either *good* business or *bad* business, and it is good or bad because it helps or does not help man to attain his final destiny which is God.

P.W., 36

C

Caesarism

Ethical Christianity has failed. Western Civilization is not just suffering from a famine of spiritual values; it is not even caring about them. It is now seeking to stuff itself with the husks of the secular, the economic, the political, the worldly. This new thing which no longer is concerned with the soul, but with the belly, is *a philosophy of life which mobilizes souls for economic and secular ends,* a Caesarism or adoration of the State, a glorification of the human collective through the depersonalization of man, and a suffocation of human personality and its subsequent absorption into the mass. Sometimes it takes only the form of a race-worship such as Nazism and at other times the form of economic worship such as Communism.

C.C., 32

Calvinist Tyranny

Calvinism . . . held that a man was determined to heaven or hell independent of his merits. As God decreed, so his destiny was fixed regardless of whether he lived well or badly. Under such a fatalism, man was not free to be a saint or to be a devil. God made him what he is, not himself.

F.G., 230

Carnality (Era of)

The world is living today in what might be described as an era of carnality, which glorifies sex, hates restraint, identifies purity with coldness, innocence with ignorance, and turns men and women into Buddhas with their eyes closed, hands folded across their breasts, intently looking inward, thinking only of self.

C.B., 39

Cartesians

Understanding became identified with measure, from which they conclude that the immeasurable is the unknowable, and the unknowable is the unreal.

G.C., 37

Cathedrals

Just as the cathedral was the center of the political and social life of the time, so the Real Presence was the center and soul of the cathedral. As man, the microcosm, summed up all visible creation within himself, whose vital principle was a soul, so too the cathedral summed up all creation within itself, and its soul was the Eucharistic Emmanuel. The world is a great sacrament and the cathedral is a still greater one. The cathedral synthetized everything. All kingdoms, the mineral, the vegetable, the animal, the human, and the angelic—all arts, all sciences, all times—left their trace on it.

O.E., 142–143

Catholic

. . . once the Catholic accepts the eternal truths of Christ, he is free to accept all the nonessential beliefs he pleases. He can be a monarchist or a republican; he can live solitary and alone on a pillar like Simon, or he can busy himself on the streets of Paris like a Vincent de Paul; he can accept Einstein or reject him; he can believe in the gold standard or the silver standard; he can play cards and dance, or he can abstain from them; he can drink moderately or he can be prohibitionist. He is like a man living on a great island in the sea on which he may roam and exercise his freedom in a thousand and one games, but only on condition that he obey the only law that is posted there: Do not jump over the walls.

C.C., 133

Catholics prefer the unchangeable truth that man has an unchangeable head; but we do not care a snap of our fingers what kind of hat he wears; he can change that to suit the fashions; but for the life of us, we cannot understand the world that wants to change its God because it discovers a new astronomy.

C.C., 134

A Catholic may sin and sin as badly as anyone else, but no genuine Catholic ever denies he is a sinner. A Catholic wants his sins forgiven—not excused or sublimated.

L.A., 149

Catholic (Bad)

The very fact that the world is a thousand times more scandalized at a bad Catholic in public life than a bad anything else, is only a proof that the world expected much more of him.

C.C., 212

Catholicism

This is the great beauty of the Catholic Faith: its sense of proportion, or balance, or should we say, its humor. It does not handle the problem of death to the exclusion of sin, nor the problem of pain to the exclusion of matter; nor the problem of sin, to the exclusion of human freedom, nor the social use of property to the exclusion of personal right; nor the reality of the body and sex to the exclusion of the soul and its function, nor the reality of matter to the forgetfulness of the Spirit.

P.R., 190

Catholicism and Dogmas

A dogma, then, is the necessary consequence of the intolerance of first principles, and that science or that church which has the greatest amount of dogmas is the science or the church that has been doing the most thinking. The Catholic Church, the schoolmaster for twenty centuries, has been doing a tremendous amount of solid, hard thinking and hence has built up dogmas as a man might build a house of brick but grounded on a rock.

O.E., 114

Catholics and America

It is our solemn duty as Catholics to be conscious of our duty to America, and to preserve its freedom by preserving its faith in God against that group that would identify revolution with America; we must protest that there are stars in our flag and not a hammer and a sickle, to remind us that the destiny of human life is beyond the implements of daily toil—beyond the stars and the "hid battlements of eternity" with God.

L.E., 135

Cause

In history, the only causes that die are those for which men refuse to die.

T.M., 8–9

Celebrity

. . . anyone who steps into a shower, where he cannot carry his press-clippings, knows that his celebrity has not elevated him above other men.

W.H., 107

Celibacy

From a psychological point of view, celibacy is not a negation of the sexual instinct, but the transformation of the libido. The transformation does not take place when the libido is solicited or directed to *without*, but when the object of love is *within*. When pulled from the outside, the spirit loses its mastery.

M.P., 325–326

Celibacy is not the renouncing of a person outside us, but the concentration on a Person inside. Celibacy is not the renouncing of love; it is the resolution to love as Christ loves.

M.P., 328

Character

Character is not revealed when life shows its best side, but when it shows its worst.

D.L., 81

Character building should not be based solely on the eradiction of evil, for it should stress even more the cultivation of virtue. Mere asceticism without love of God is pride; it is possible to concentrate so hard on humiliating ourselves that we become proud of our humility, and to concentrate so intently on eradicating evil as to make our purity nothing but a condemnation of others.

O.B., 105

A man's real good is that which he works most earnestly to preserve, and which saddens him most when he loses it.

W.I., 15

Charity

The way to win friends and influence people is not to flatter them, but to be selfless. The greatest happiness in life comes not from having, but from giving. From the Christian point of view the true master is the servant.

L.A., 114

Asceticism and mortification are not the ends of a Christian life; they are only the means. The end is charity.

O.B., 105

Charity is a habit, not a gush, or sentiment; it is a virtue, not an ephemeral thing of moods and impulses; it is a quality of the soul, rather than an isolated good deed.

P.R., 222

Charity (Modern)

The . . . tendency in modern charity, if we are correctly observing contemporary movement, is towards greater organization, even to the extent of making it one of the big business concerns of the country. The bread-basket stage, the penny-in-a-tin-cup stage, the hand-out stage, have given way to the bureau and the scientific-giving stage. Statistics are replacing sympathy, and social workers are replacing emotions.

O.E., 233

Chastity (Vow of)

. . . the vow of chastity releases the flesh not only from the narrow and circumscribed family where there can still be selfishness, but also for the service of that family which embraces all humanity. That is why the Church asks those who consecrate themselves to the redemption of the world to take a vow and to surrender all selfishness, that they may belong to no one family and yet belong to all.

C.B., 44

Cheerfulness

Cheerfulness is that quality which enables one to make others happy. It takes its origin half in personal goodness, and half in the belief of the personal goodness of others. It is the opposite of the morbid, the morose, the fretful, the grumbling, the somber.

G.T., 147

Chesterton, G. K.

Since my life has covered such a long span, it has undergone several influences in style. The greatest influence in writing was G. K. Chesterton, who never used a useless word, who saw the value of a paradox and avoided what was trite.

A., 79

Childlike

Childlikeness is not childishness. To be childish is to retain in maturity what should have been discarded at the threshold of manhood. Childlikeness, on the contrary, implies that with the mental breadth and practical strength and wisdom of maturity, there is associated the humility, trustfulness, spontaneity, and obedience of the child.

O.B., 173

Children

Lenin once said that he cared not how many people in Russia over fifty opposed Communism; all he wanted were the children.

D.L., 87

. . . in the Divine solicitude for children was the affirmation that there are certain elements in childhood which ought to be preserved in the highest manhood; that no man is truly great unless he can recapture something of the simplicity and humility of the child.

D.L., 88

The first question a child asks when he comes into this world is the question: Why? Every babe is an incipient philosopher.

R.G., 327

The child is . . . the sign and promise of human liberty, because he is a new act of freedom added to the world.

T.M., 225

Children (Delinquent)

The root of this trouble is in the *home;* and those who talk about more nurseries, better playgrounds, curfews, better milk, and more dance halls, are perhaps diminishing the effect but not removing the cause.

S.P., 81

Choice

This is the choice before us: either try to revolutionize the world and break under it or revolutionize ourselves and remake the world.

E.I., 47

By consenting to every common impulse and the pleasure of every sense, one becomes a "Yes-man" to the voice of self-destruction. Our character is made by our choices.

L.A., 96

Christendom

We are living at the end of Christendom—not the end of Christianity. By Christendom is meant the political, economic and social order pervaded by the Gospel ethic. We no longer live in a Christian civilization. Christendom refers only to the world and its institutions; Christianity refers to Christ and His Mystical Body in its evident outreach to the world. The era of Faith was succeeded by the era of Reason, which, in turn, has given way to our Sensate Age. Christianity is considered off the reservation.

M.P., 138

Christian

To be worthy of the name Christian, then, means that we, too, must thirst for the spread of the Divine Love; and if we do not thirst, then we shall never be invited to sit down at the banquet of Life.

R.S., 70

To every Christian . . . there comes the supreme moment when he must choose between temporal pleasure and eternal freedom. In order to save our souls, we must often run the risk of losing our bodies.

R.S., 97

. . . the more Christian we become, the more God-fearing we are, the more we insist on morality in education, family life and politics, the more we will be regarded with suspicion and with hate. Our very existence will be regarded as a danger. We need do nothing to bring a reaction against us, any more than the early Christians of Rome, who were good citizens, were guilty of any other crime than that of refusing to call Nero "Fuehrer" or god.

S.P., 73

The true followers of Christ were meant to be at odds with the world: The pure of heart will be laughed at by the Freudians; the meek will be scorned by the Marxists; the humble will be walked on by the go-getters; the liberal Sadducees will call them reactionaries; the reactionary Pharisees will call them liberals.

S.V., 25

Christianity

Has Christianity failed? The answer is: If by the term *Christianity* is meant that vague ethical humanism which has repudiated practically all the divine elements in Christianity, then Christianity has failed.

C.C., 18–19

Christianity does not begin by reforming society; it begins by regenerating men.

M.W., 62

Christianity and Science

Christianity, by emphasizing discipline, reason, and the value of nature as such, became the rock on which empirical science was founded. Science arose and could arise only in a Christian civilization. The East, lacking this foundation, never became scientific.

L.4, 94

Science is not inimical to a Christian civilization, for it has flourished only in a Christian civilization. It has not flourished in a Buddhist civilization, nor amongst the Mohammedans, for the reason that a pantheistic civilization that confuses God and the world can never get hold of the world alone to study it scientifically. The Christian conception, on the contrary, makes God and the world distinct, and therefore makes it possible for a man to study the universe as the universe. In doing this, man follows out the injunction of the Creator, Who commanded man to rule over the earth and subject it.

O.E., 156

Christianity (Decline of)

The disintegration of Christianity is not to be laid at the door of the Jews. Those who had most influence in robbing minds of the Divinity of Christ, by ridicule, slander, or by denying His existence, were not Jews: Voltaire, Rousseau, Hume, Kant, Hegel, Schleiermacher, Schopenhauer, Feuerbach, Friedrich Strauss, Neitzsche, Buechner, Haeckel, Drews, and the thousand lesser lights of today.

L.A., 127

Christians and Anti-Semitism

No Christian hates the Jews because of the Crucifixion related in the Gospels—any more than the British hate the Americans because of the Declaration of Independence.

L.A., 132

Christians and Jews

There is no Jew in the world who loves God and hates Christians, and there is no Christian in the world who truly loves God-made-man and hates Jews. Anti-Christianity and anti-Semitism are the yardsticks of our mutual failure to be religious.

L.A., 134

The Jew and the Christian begin to hate one another at that moment when both look for *external* causes of their misery, the Jew putting all the blame on the Christian story of the Crucifixion, and the Christian putting all the blame on the Jews.

The Jew and the Christian begin to love one another when both look for the *internal* causes of their misery; that is, their sins and their forgetfulness of the moral law of God.

L.A., 134

Christians (Liberal)

Liberal Christianity has too long assumed that it is the sole business of the Church to beat the drums for social reform and to dance to the tunes piped for it by the latest moods and passing mental fashions.

D.V., 19

Liberal Christianity which thinks of God solely as a God of sentimental love—such love as a doting modern mother might have for her erring son who could do no wrong, and even when he did it, must needs be forgiven, for he did not mean it.

D.V., 19

Christmas

Christmas is not for sophomores who live under the illusion that they read all of Darwin, or for the intelligentsia . . . or for the self-wise who think Marx is wiser than Mark. It is only for the very learned, the great scientists, the profound theologians who are heirs of the wise men who discovered Wisdom. At the other end of the spectrum are the simple people who know nature better than books, who have insights deeper than the impure and a vision which sees in the night. These are the heirs of the shepherds who find their way to the Shepherd of their souls.

C.I., 34

There were only two classes of men who heard the cry that night: Shepherds and Wise Men. Shepherds: those who know they know nothing. Wise Men: those who know they do not know everything.

D.R., 71

Christmas which was once a feast, has become a festival.

M.P., 81

If Christmas were just the birthday of a great teacher, like Socrates or Buddha, it would never have split time into two, so that all history before the advent of Christ is called B.C. and all history after, A.D.

O.B., 228

The Church

The notice of her execution has been posted, but the execution has never taken place. Science killed her, and still she was there; History interred her, but still she was alive. Modernism slew her, but still she lived.

D.R., 138

If we Catholics believed all the lies and calumnies that are told about the Church, we would hate it ten times more than bigots do. The enemies of the Church often do not hate the Church: they only hate what they erroneously believe to be the Church.

L.A., 142

Judge the Catholic Church not by those who barely live by its spirit, but by the example of those who live closest to it.

L.A., 147

. . . it never suits the particular mood of any age, because it was made for all ages.

A Catholic knows that if the Church married the mood of any age in which it lived, it would be a widow in the next age. The mark of the true Church is that it will never get on well with the passing moods of the world: "I have chosen you out of the world, therefore the world hateth you." (John 15:19)

L.A., 149

Today she is accused of being behind the times because she does not go mad about Freud, and I dare say, that in fifty years from now, if one of the teachers in any of our great universities mounted his rostrum and talked Freud, he would be considered just as antiquated and behind the times as a politician who today might mount a soap-box at the corner of 42nd and Broadway, and open a campaign for William McKinley as President.

M.T., 205

A man can join any other movement, group, or cult without provoking hostile comment from his neighbors and friends; he can even found some esoteric sun cult of his own and be tolerated as a citizen exercising his legitimate freedom and satisfying his own religious needs. But as soon as anyone joins the Church, hatred, opposition appear.

P.S., 261

The Church is not a continuous phenomenon through history. Rather, it is something that has been through a thousand resurrections after a thousand crucifixions. The bell is always sounding for its execution which, by some great power of God, is everlastingly postponed.

T.M., 221

It is not for the Church we have to fear, but for the world.

W.W., 118

The Church and Politics

If by interference in politics is meant judging or condemning a philosophy of life which makes the party, or the state, or the class, or the race the source of all rights, and which usurps the soul and enthrones party over conscience and denies those basic rights for which this war was fought, the answer is emphatically *Yes!* The Church does judge such a philosophy. But when it does this, it is not interfering with politics, for such politics is no longer politics but Theology. When a State sets itself up as absolute as God, when it claims sovereignty over the soul, when it destroys freedom of conscience and freedom of religion, then the State has ceased to be political and has begun to be a counter-Church.

C.P., 36

What is the attitude of much of the world today in the midst of war? Note the change! For the past fifty years the world said: "We want no spiritual authority," but for the past two years it asks: "Why does not your spiritual authority have more authority?" The world spent one hundred and fifty years exiling a spiritual force from international relations, and now is angry because that same spiritual force has not kept peace in the house from which it was exiled. The very ones who some twenty years ago did all they could to make the Church weak, now bemoan because it is not strong.

P.W., 180–181

The Church and Property

Because the abolition of property is the beginning of slavery, the Church is opposed to Capitalism which concentrates property in the hands of the few, and to Communism which confiscates it all in the name of the collectivity. Being profoundly interested in the liberty of man, the Church takes the practical step of suggesting that which will make him free; namely, give him something he can call his own.

F.G., 44

The Church and Reason

The Church is accused of being the enemy of reason; as a matter of fact, she is the only one who believes in it. Using her reason in the Council of the Vatican, she officially went on record in favor of Rationalism, and declared, against the mock humility of the Agnostics and the sentimental faith of the Fideists, that human reason by its own power can know something besides the contents of test-tubes and retorts, and that working on mere sensible phenomena it can soar even to the "hid battlements of eternity."

O.E., 9

Church and State

We could not have a union of Church and State in America without a complete change in the Constitution and the Bill of Rights.

And if a radical change of the Constitution were contemplated, we can assure the alarmists that the greater opposition to that change would come from the Catholics themselves.

W.W., 85–86

The Church (Tragedy of)

The tragedy of the Church is that so many of these zealous souls in earnest love of the world became secular in spirit. Having started with the world, they moved backward and used the Church as a whipping post, and Christ to justify any position they held. They *used* Jesus. He did not *use them*. Hence, countless pamphlets on "Jesus and homosexuals," "Jesus and Amnesty," "Jesus and Sex," "Jesus and the Rebels," "Jesus and Revolution." Their commitment to Him becomes only skin deep because they "play it safe." In the rightful fervor for social dimension, the Christ-depth was lost.

M.P., 246

The Church versus Marxists

. . . the Church's protest against economic injustices cuts far deeper than that of the Marxists. The tragedy of a thwarted economic life to a Marxist is that he cannot be a full animal; the tragedy to the Church is that he cannot be a free man.

W.W., 70

Circumcision

Circumcision in the Old Testament was a prefiguring of Baptism in the New Testament. Both symbolize a renunciation of the flesh with its sins. The first was done by wounding of the body; the second, by cleansing the soul. The first incorporated the child into the body of Israel; the second incorporates the child into the body of the new Israel or the Church.

L.C., 37

Circumstance

The major difference between human beings is not in what happens to them, but in how they react to what happens. Blindness makes some bitter; others, like Helen Keller, it makes apostles of inspiration.

D.L., 81

Civilization

Civilization is not to be identified with commercial prestige but with moral worth; not with goods, but with goodness.

C.C., 183

Civilization and Salvation

It is not our economics which have failed; it is man who has failed —man who has forgotten God. Hence no manner of economic or political readjustment can possibly save our civilization; we can be saved only by a renovation of the inner man, only by a purging of our hearts and souls; for only by seeking first the Kingdom of God and His Justice will all these other things be added unto us.

P., 5

Classes of People

There are in the sight of God only two classes of people; the once-born and the twice-born; those who are born of woman, and those who are born of the spirit of God. The first are just men; the second are children of God; the first are humanists, the second are Christians; the first are of the world, the second are of the kingdom of God.

M.B., 235

Clothing

Clothing therefore tells the story of inner and outer worth. It is a symbol of lost innocence, a memento of a former glory. There are therefore two fashions: the passing fashion of the world and the enduring fashion of the spiritual. In the final reckoning it will not matter how we are dressed on the outside; one can go into the Kingdom of Heaven in rags; but it makes an eternity of difference as to how we are dressed on the inside.

L. 5, 240

Cockroach versus Man

The cockroach, which according to one's measurement has "remained unchanged for more than fifty million years," has seen many things evolve under his very eye. He has perhaps even seen bug-dynasties and flea-kingdoms rise and fall according to the Spenglerian formula, but the cockroach in all that fifty million years has never formulated even the simplest explanation of evolution that a man might formulate in an hour. It is that power to contain within his mind the infinitely great cosmos, and the infinitely little atom, and the infinite variety between the two, and to think of them all in the one thought—Order—that makes man the "beauty of the world and the paragon of animals."

O.E., 26

Collectivists

Their hatred is weakness, for it refuses to see that collective selfishness is just as wrong as individual selfishness; it is the weakness of the man who is not self-possessed, who uses his fist instead of his mind, who resorts to violence for the same reason the ignorant man resorts to blasphemy; namely, because he has not sufficient intellectual strength to express himself otherwise.

C.B., 12

Collectivity

. . . the totalitarian views of Nazism, Fascism and Communism are wrong for they assume that the individual man is intrinsically corrupt and can be made tame, docile and obedient only by the force of the collectivity enshrined in a dictator.

P.R., 37

College Courses

Education should not be based on the substitution of one idea by another, but on the deepening and widening of a single body of knowledge and understanding. Education does not mean the substitution of Freud for James, James for Spencer; nor the substitution of Baltemann for Harnach and Harnach for Strauss; nor the substitution of Eddington for Rutherford and Rutherford for Feuerbach. Rather, knowledge is like life, which grows from unity to multiplicity, just as the oak unfolds the mystery of the acorn. College courses should be so constructed as to give those basic principles and disciplines which will unfold and deepen all through life.

L.5, 275

Comedian

The most honest of those who appear on radio or television, as regards their material, are the comedians. . . . The comedians admit, though they speak the humorous lines, that they actually are indebted to others for putting them in their mouths. One never sees on a television screen at the end of a program given by a politician the name of the one who wrote his speech.

T.T., 92

Commandments

When you buy an automobile, the manufacturer gives you a set of instructions. He tells you the pressure to which you ought to inflate your tires, the kind of oil you ought to use in the crankcase, and the proper fuel to put in the gas tank. He has nothing against you by giving you these instructions as God had nothing against you in giving you commandments. The manufacturer wants to be helpful; he is anxious that you get the maximum utility out of the car. And God is anxious that we get the maximum happiness out of life. Such is the purpose of His commandments.

P.R., 38

Communism

. . . is a complete philosophy of life, what the Germans called a *Weltanschauung,* an integral comprehension of the world, different from all other secular systems in that it seeks not only to dominate the periphery of life but to control man's inner life as well. Communism has a theory and a practice; it wishes to be not only a state but a church judging the consciences of men; it is a doctrine of salvation and as such claims the whole man, body and soul, and in this sense is totalitarian.

C.C., 58

The only place in the world where communism works is in a convent, for there the basis of having everything in common is that no one wants anything. Communism has not worked in Moscow, but it does work in a monastery.

L.A., 103–104

. . . it is Communism which is the ally of capitalism in carrying its abuses to the point where it substitutes a few red bureaucrats for a few capitalists. Communism is capitalism gone mad.

L.E., 19

Communism is the final logic of the dehumanization of man.

L.2, 122

Communism is not merely an economic doctrine. It is more properly a philosophy of life which mobilizes souls for economic and secular ends; a Caesarism or adoration of the State; a glorification of the human collective through the de-personalization of men; a suffocation of human personality and its subsequent absorption into the mass; a filtering of barbarism through the sieve of the class, the race, or the state, and calling it Civilization.

P., 23

Communism and Nazism

Their conflict is not one of ideologies, for Communism and Nazism are both destructive of human freedom.

P.W., 7

Communism and the Masses

But despite its raucous appeal to what it calls the proletariat, the masses of America are untouched by Communist propaganda. They were not fooled, but the intelligentsia were. Communism has won more recruits in one single University in New York than it has won among all the farm hands of Illinois and Iowa put together.

G.C., 42

Communism versus Christianity

In contrast to this Christian philosophy of forgiveness, there exists for the first time in the history of the world a philosophy and a political and social system based not on love, but on hate, and that is Communism. Communism believes that the only way it can establish itself is by inciting revolution, class-struggle, and violence. Hence its regime is characterized by a hatred of those who believe the family is the basic unit of society. The very Communistic gesture of the clenched fist is a token of its pugnacious and destructive spirit, and a striking contrast indeed to the nailed hand of the Saviour pleading forgiveness for the clenched-fisted generation who sent Him to the Cross.

C.B., 11

Communist

If Communists used as much violence on their selfishness as they use on others, they would all be saints!

C.B., 12

Every Communist is a Capitalist without any cash in his pockets; he is an involuntary Capitalist.

S.P., 54

Compassion

Emptiness as regards the self, is balanced by compassion for others. The less stress on the ego, the more care there is for neighbor. At the moment St. Francis emptied himself of his possessions, he made himself free for compassion.

M.P., 46–47

Compassion (Modern)

The new compassion that has crept into our courts and into our literature and drama is the compassion for the breakers of the law, for the thieves, the dope fiends, the murderers, the rapists. This false compassion for the criminal and the readiness to blame the law and the police, has passed from the "sob-sisters" to black-robed justices who, fearful of restraining a liberty turned into license, pardon the mugger and ignore the mugged.

G.T., 133

Compulsion

It has been stated that flammable material exists on the inside of every human being. For example, the righteous use of sex could be perverted into grossness; a desire for perfection could turn one into a tyrant; and the desire for property as the extension of oneself, into a miser. The stages by which one advances into compulsion are: first, the consent of the will to any temptation; next, the act which is the result of the temptation; and, finally, the habit itself.

It takes many acts to make a habit, as it takes many strands of flax to make a rope.

G.T., 15

Democracies boast that they alone have freedom, because they do not force their people to submit to a dictatorship. But there are psychologists, psychiatrists, philosophers, dramatists in democracy who deny that when a man does anything wrong he is guilty. "Compulsion" is the polite word to cover up the denial of inner freedom.

O.B., 161

Confession

The people who are dragging their shame into a confessional box, with their feet hanging out from under a curtain like wiggling worms, have courage to face their own shame. It is the cowards who are running off to pillboxes, and to a thousand and one other escapes, who have not the courage to face that which has within themselves the possibility of great dignity.

O.B., 47

Confessions of St. Augustine

In 397, or twelve years after his conversion, Augustine wrote his *Confessions*, the greatest spiritual autobiography ever written. It is the work of a teacher who explains, a philosopher who thinks, a theologian who instructs, a poet who achieves chaste beauty in the writing, and a mystic who pours out thanks for having found himself in peace. None of the Freuds or Jungs or Adlers of our generation has ever pierced the conscious and the unconscious mind with a rapier as keen as Augustine's. No man can say he has ever understood himself if he has not read the *Confessions of Augustine*.

L.5, 258

Conscience

There was a preacher once who was saying to the congregation, "It is wrong to steal horses." The congregation answered, "Amen, amen." "It is wrong to steal cows." "Amen! Amen!" Then he said, "It is wrong to steal chickens." And someone shouted back, "Now he is meddling." Up to that point, conscience was not touched.

L.4, 5

The voice of conscience can be stilled in four ways: by killing it, by denying it, by drowning it, and by fleeing from it.

P.S., 91

When night gives our inner vision scope, the guilty conscience lies awake, fearful of being known in all its ugliness. There is nothing that so arouses unhealthy fear as a hidden guilt.

P.S., 94

. . . consciences only sleep, they never die.

W.I., 41

The universal norm of morality which is conscience, is rooted in human nature and therefore is the same for all men. Its inner voice fills me with a sense of responsibility, telling me not that I *must* do something, but I *ought* to do something, for the difference between a machine and a man is the difference of freedom.

W.W., 29

Conscience (Examination of)

What . . . materialists threw out of the front door some psychiatrists now sneak in through the back door under a new name—examination of the unconscious.

P.S., 79

Consolation

Consolation is in explaining suffering, not forgetting it; in relating it to Love, not ignoring it; in making it an expiation for sin, not another sin.

S.V., 23

Contentment

Contentment is not an innate virtue. It is acquired through great resolution and diligence in conquering unruly desires; hence it is an art which few study.

W.H., 15

Contraception

Shall we not say in justice, then, that the man and woman who take the gift of love into their hearts, and then turn it against producing life, for the selfishness of their own pleasure, are betraying life and love's great trust, stealing heaven's fire, and enkindling the flame which consumes them and leaves naught but their dust behind? Why, even though such a couple did not believe in God, even though they believed only in love, their own hearts of hearts should tell them that love was meant to be recovered in life, and that to be unfaithful to that gift of love, and refuse to increase life, is to live in a world in which artists are always picking up brushes but never finishing a picture; always lifting chisels but never producing a statue; always touching bow to string, but never emitting a harmony.

H.C., 68

Contradiction

God cannot do anything which would contradict His nature, not in the sense that He is bound by anything outside Himself, but because His nature is justice itself.

M.U., 30

Control

It is one of the curious anomalies of present-day civilization that when man achieves greatest control over nature, he has the least control over himself. The great boast of our age is our domination of the universe: we have harnessed the waterfalls, made the wind a slave to carry us on wings of steel, and squeezed from the earth the secret of its age. Yet, despite this mastery of nature, there perhaps never was a time when man was less a master of himself. He is equipped like a veritable giant to control the forces of nature, but is as weak as a pigmy to control the forces of his passions and inclinations.

M.U., 49

Conversation

There has never been a person who monopolized a conversation without at the same time monotonizing it.

T.T., 169

Conversion

Paul had to begin with the Cross and then retrace his steps backward to Calvary. To him and to his people, the prophetic connection between suffering and glory were repugnant. The Jew and the Greek both had a horror of death; to the Greek there was a physical aversion; to the Jew it was a moral shame. And yet the glorified Christ began Paul's conversion with the Cross—at that very point where all national characteristics were assailed. He had to see Christ repersecuted, recrucified, renailed. And when he asked who it was who questioned, there flashed the vision: "I am Jesus, Whom you are persecuting" (Acts 26:16).

M.P., 108

Though there be such things as deathbed conversions, nevertheless as the tree falls, there it lies. One man who led an evil life always boasted of the fact that he needed never worry about his soul when time would end, for he could save it with three words which he quoted in Latin: *"Miserere mei Deus."* He was right about saying three words at the moment of his death, but they were not the words he expected to say, for his life had not been so lived as to pronounce them from his heart. As his horse threw him over the cliff he said: *"Capiat omnia diabolus,"* which means, "I'll be damned."

O.B., 234

Conversions are not more difficult in our times than before; but the approach must be different. Today, people are looking for God, not because of the order they find in the universe, but because of the disorder they find in themselves. They are coming to God through an inner disgust, a despair that may be called creative.

P.N., 5–7

Before conversion, it was behavior which to a large extent determined belief; after conversion, it is belief which determines behavior.

P.S., 251

Counselling

Counselling is touching where there is disease or misfortune; it is not the simple giving of advice.

P.N., 155

Counting

There is nothing which so much dulls the human spirit as counting . . .

D.L., 48

Courtesy

Courtesy is not a condescension of a superior to an inferior, or a patronizing interest in another's affairs. It is the homage of the heart to the sacredness of human worth.

D.L., 50

Courtesy is affection and not affectation. It reaches a point where, in a true lowliness of mind, one esteems others better than self. We know the worst that is in us and of that we can be certain, but we can never know the worst that is in others; we can at best only suspect it. Conscious of this, our feelings toward others become delicate and sensitive; they may even become deeply religious when they reach a point where we forgive others their discourtesies.

O.B., 178

. . . it is the giving to everyone his human due as interpreted by love. It is not something that is learned at a charm school, but rather is the sister of charity which banishes hatred and cherishes love.

O.B., 179

Creating

To create is to recognize the spirit in things; to imitate is to submerge personality at the lowest level of the mass.

O.B., 190

Genesis tells us that after the creation of the world, *"God saw all that he had made, and found it very good."* Such contemplation of his work is natural to man, whenever he, too, is engaged in a creative task.

W.H., 55

Creation

God created the world for something like the same reason that we find it hard to keep a secret! Good things are hard to keep. The rose is good, and tells its secret in perfume. The sun is good, and tells its secret in light and heat. Man is good, and tells the secret of his goodness in the language of thought. But God is Infinitely Good, and therefore Infinitely Loving. Why therefore could not He by a free impulse of His Love let love overflow and bring new worlds into being? God could not keep, as it were, the secret of His Love, and the telling of it was Creation.

D.R., 41–42

Credibility

Credibility and behavior are twins. Only the man who practices his convictions is believable. Otherwise they are like announcers urging the viewer to buy a Chevrolet while they drive a Plymouth. There was some truth in the cry of Bonhoeffer during the Nazi days: "Only he who cries out in defense of the Jews dare permit himself to sing Gregorian!"

M.P., 88

Creeds

The passing of creeds and dogmas means the passing of controversies. Creeds and dogmas are social; prejudices are private. Believers bump into one another at a thousand different angles, but bigots keep out of one another's way, because prejudice is anti-social. I can imagine an old-fashioned Calvinist who holds that the word "damn" has a tremendous dogmatic significance, coming to intellectual blows with an old-fashioned Methodist who holds that it is only a curse word; but I cannot imagine a controversy if both decide to damn damnation, like our Modernists who no longer believe in Hell.

O.E., 5

We fit a creed to the way we live, rather than the way we live to a creed; we suit religion to our actions, rather than actions to religion. We try to keep religion on a speculative basis in order to avoid moral reproaches on our conduct. We sit at the piano of life and insist that every note we strike is right—because we struck it.

We justify want of faith by saying, "I don't go to Church, but I am better than those who do."

P.S., 101

Crisis

The world is never without crisis, for crisis means a judgment on the way it lives and thinks and acts toward others. Every crisis is a rehearsal for the final judgment.

D.L., 183

All crises, even those of material disaster, force the soul inward.

P.S., 221

Critic

Critics are often men who have failed.

D.L., 117

. . . there are no monuments in the world built for critics.

D.L., 127

There is not a critical person in the world who is not in need of criticism.

D.L., 134

Criticism

Not always, but sometimes, criticism is the outcome of an incapacity to produce, or a defense against one's own inferiority.

D.L., 117

. . . the habit of criticism is the best indication of an incomplete life.

s.w., 82

The Cross

The Cross is evil at its worst and Goodness at its best.

L.4, 240

The Christ without the Cross cannot save, for He stands for effeminancy, permissiveness and Jesus the Superstar who uses music to solace defeat. The Cross without Christ cannot save, for it stands for Dachau, Auschwitz, concentration camps, the crushing of individuals like grapes to make the collective wine of the state.

M.P., 33

Most lives are frustrated because they have left out the Cross.

s.w., 81

Crown of Thorns

The crown of thorns is the condition of the crown of glory.

O.B., 221

Crucifix

The sight of a crucifix has a continuity with Golgotha; at times its vision is embarrassing. We can keep a statue of Buddha in a room, tickle his tummy for good luck, but it is never mortifying. The crucifix somehow or other, makes us feel involved. It is much more than a picture of Marie Antoinette and the death-dealing guillotine. No matter how much we thrust it away, it makes its plaguing reappearance like an unpaid bill.

M.P., 101–102

The Crucifixion

. . . the sun refused to shine on the crucifixion! The light that rules the day, probably for the first and last time in history, was snuffed out like a candle when, according to every human calculation, it should have continued to shine. The reason was that the crowning crime of man, the killing of nature's Lord, could not pass without a protest from nature itself.

S.L., 32

The Cross is not something that *has* happened; the Crucifixion is something that *is* happening. It can be found at any place and at any hour in the human race, for it is the epic struggle of the forces of good and evil.

T.T., 190

The death of Our Lord on the Cross reveals that we are meant to be perpetually dissatisfied here below. If earth were meant to be a Paradise, then He Who made it would never have taken leave of it on Good Friday. The commending of the Spirit to the Father was at the same time the refusal to commend it to earth. The completion or fulfillment of life is in heaven, not on earth.

V.V., 99

Culture

Culture today is becoming politicized. The modern State is extending dominance over areas outside its province, family, education, and the soul. It is concentrating public opinion in fewer and fewer hands, which becomes the more dangerous because of the mechanical way in which propaganda can be disseminated. It seeks to achieve its ends by extra parliamentary means. The idea of a community of workers is replaced by mass cooperation on a non-personal basis; contract has taken the place of responsibility. The lines are becoming clear-cut.

C.P., 38

Cutting Corners

The justification for cutting corners, taking bribes and other forms of dishonesty is twofold. First is, "Everybody's doing it." The assumption here is that right and wrong are questions merely of mob judgment, rather than of standards. It forgets that right is right if nobody is right, and wrong is wrong if everybody is wrong.

G.T., 124

Cynic

A cynic is a man who cheats at solitaire and then thinks that everyone else in the world is a cheat.

T.T., 14

Cynicism

Another escape hatch for unadmitted guilt is cynicism. The difference between the pessimist and the cynic is that the pessimist carries on the losing battle against life in his own soul, while the cynic tries to wage the battle in someone else's soul. His own inner defeat, the cynic projects onto others; because he is unhappy, he tries to make them unhappy by ridiculing the basis of their inner peace. His joy is to "debunk" others, because he has already "debunked" himself. Such a person tries to free himself from guilt by projecting it onto his neighbor.

L.H., 15

D

Damnation

We lose our souls not only because we do evil things, but because we neglect to do good: the buried talent, the unmarked second mile, the passing by the wounded. How often in the Gospel condemnation follows because "we did nothing" (Matthew 25:42–46).

M.P., 178

Darkness

More men discover their souls in darkness than they do in light. This is not to invite darkness; it is only to be reminded that darkness need not go to waste when it is thrust upon us.

O.B., 49

Darwinism

. . . to confuse Darwinism with evolution is like confusing bal-
loon-trousers with pants. A man may be an evolutionist without
being Darwinian, just as a man may be civilized without wearing
lace sleevelets. There are, it must be remembered, about 57 vari-
eties of evolution, most of which are more or less acceptable working hypotheses in the empirical order. Evolution is a much bigger
problem than the one that asks which came first, the monkey or
the organ-grinder.

O.E., 304

Day-care

In vain does one say that the function of teaching can be fulfilled
adequately by the state, for the state cannot be nurse in every nurs-
ery, nor the government the governess in every playroom. There is
only one place where the human tradition can be developed, and
that is the home: there are only two persons who can love those
whom the state does not think worth loving, and they are the
father and mother.

M.U., 72

Death

In the Victorian era, sex was taboo. In our era of homosexuality,
fornication and carnality, death is taboo. The vestiges of death are
swept away as silently and unostentatiously as possible. Death is
not to be mentioned in polite society; its shadow casts a gloom
over the god Eros. The quest for pleasure and the release of ten-
sions produced a Dionysian culture that stresses ecstasy, revelry,
license!

M.P., 162

Animals die, and so do men, but the difference is that men *know* they *must* die. By that very fact, we men surmount death, we get above it, we transcend it, look at it, survey it, and thus stand *outside* it. This very act is a dim foreshadowing of immortality. Our mortality is frightening to us largely because we can contemplate *immortality,* and we have a dim suspicion that we have lost the immortality that once belonged to us.

P.S., 198–199

Death and the Media

Hidden in the media's love of the tragic is not only a hidden death-wish, but also an unconscious concern with the ultimate: death. Accidents, muggings, assassinations are interesting as penultimates because they avoid facing the ultimate. The same is true of the passion for revolution and the despisal of the past. One would almost think to hear the revolutionists speak that they were born without navels—having no debt or bond or cord to the past. For the first time they no longer think about history, so as to avoid old errors with new labels; rather, they seek consciously to create history as a "now."

M.P., 116

Decay

Revolting books against virtue are termed "courageous"; those against morality are advertised as "daring and forward-looking"; and those against God are called "progressive and epoch-making." It has always been the characteristic of a generation in decay to paint the gates of hell with the gold of paradise.

M.U., 107–108

The Declaration of Independence

The Declaration of Independence is no more a finished thing than birth; it is an original endowment like life, which is progressive through moral effort and obedience to law.

W.W., 69

Defection

. . . in many cases those who lost the faith never did so for a *reason*. They left it for a *thing*. Souls generally do not fall away from Christ because of the Creed; they first have difficulty with the Commandments. The Creed, later on, becomes the handy tool of their rationalization: "I no longer believe in confession."

M.P., 76

Deism

Rationalism was not solely negative, in eliminating the supernatural and Providence; in its constructive moments it built up a religion in perfect keeping with its rationalist principles: a religion based uniquely upon reason and principles of reason—the religion of deism.

P.O., 12

Democracy

Democracy is a very Christian doctrine, the theological basis of which is the brotherhood of men and the Fatherhood of God.

C.C., 61

A democracy flirts with the danger of becoming a slave state in direct ratio to the numbers of its citizens who work, but do not own; or who own, but do not work; or who distribute, as politicians do but do not produce.

O.B., 140

The State exists for the person; not the person for the State.
Democracy is founded on this moral principle. Totalitarianism in all its forms, on the contrary, believes the person exists for the State.

S.P., 60

The *principle* of democracy is a recognition of the sovereign, inalienable rights of man as a gift of God, the Source of law.

W.W., 60

Religion owes something to democracy, but democracy needs religion more than religion needs democracy. A religion can live without democracy; it can live under tyranny, persecution and dictatorship—not comfortably, it is true, but heroically and divinely. But democracy cannot live without religion, for without religion democracy will degenerate into demagogy by selling itself to the highest bidder.

W.W., 71

Democracy (American)

The gravest danger to American democracy . . . is not from the outside; it is from the inside—the hearts of citizens in whom the light of faith has gone out. Keep God as the origin of authority and you keep the ethical character of authority; reject Him and the authority becomes power subject to no law except its own.

W.W., 64

Denial

The worst thing in the world is not sin; it is the denial of sin by a false conscience—for that attitude makes forgiveness impossible.

L.H., 14

Depression

Depression comes not from having faults, but from refusing to face them. What else is self-pity but a total unconcern with the interests of others?

T.A., 78

Despair

During the last century the theory of evolution applied to sociology, resulted in the false idea of "progress" which led men to believe that cosmic laws guaranteed his necessary and inevitable perfection. In those days of progress, man had faith in tomorrow, faith in big business, faith in science, faith in utilitarian education, faith in common sense, faith in faith. When "progress" cracked, all the baseless duties of unreasonable faith collapsed, and we found ourselves not evolving but dissolving. The notion of the "inevitable" then substituted itself for "progress." Having lost the purposiveness of human life in relation to the beatific vision, faith gave way to despair.

C.C., 151

The soul that despairs never cries to God.

L.C., 380

Man alone, of all creatures, has a soul which is capable of knowing the infinite; he alone has aspirations beyond what he sees and touches and feels; he alone can attain everything in the world and still not be satisfied. That is why, when he misses the infinite and the eternal for which he was made and which alone can satisfy, he despairs.

O.B., 42

Determinism

The simple words "Thank you" will always stand out as a refutation of determinism, for they imply that something which was done could possibly have been left undone.

L.L., 23

Determinist

. . . the very individuals who deny all human responsibility and freedom in theory freely blame their cooks for burned bacon in the morning and say "Thank you" at night to the friend who praises their latest book, *There Is No Freedom*.

P.S., 141

Devil

The devil appears as the representative of good. No one does evil for the mere sake of evil. Evil is done for the seeming good that is in it. The devil knows that we are not so depraved that we want to do evil.

E.I., 77

Devolution

Apart from an outside supernatural assistance society goes from bad to worse until deterioration is universal. Not evolution but devolution is the law of man without God. . . . With all of our boasted mechanical civilization a day might come when our modern towers of Babel would be as forgotten as the first, when Americans would cease to exist as a race as the Babylonians and Medes have ceased to exist, when Washington would be a contested locality like the capital of the Aztec civilization, and when the Constitution of the United States would be the hopeless search of the world's archaeologists.

P., 8

Dictators

. . . no dictator could ever succeed in winning the masses unless he promised them liberty. He would use force, act like a tyrant, blot out all opposition, and purge minorities, but he was always careful to do it in the sacred name of liberty.

F.G., 16

. . . dictators are like boils, superficial manifestations of an inner rottenness. They would never have come to the surface if there had not been the proper conditions in the world from which they came.

G.W., 39

Diets

The Church fasts; the world diets. Materially there is no difference, for a person can lose twenty pounds one way as well as the other. But the difference is in the intention.

V.V., 62

Dilettante

Dilettante minds plant idealism one month, then pull up the tender roots to plant realism; then sow existentialism only to abort it; they discover in the end that there is no harvest.

M.P., 127

Diplomat (Soviet)

Men sometimes throw up their hands in holy horror at what is called "a woman's reason," but it is nothing compared with the double talk of the Soviets.

L.4, 270

The stupidity of talking to a brick wall is highly reasonable in comparison with talking to anyone who has come out of the Kremlin wall.

L.4, 271

Dirt

Three kinds of dirt can accumulate on the windows of the soul to keep God's light from coming in. There is a carnal dirt or sexual excesses; money dirt or lust for possessions, and egocentric dirt or selfishness and vanity.

F.D., 212

Disaster

Disaster comes from any attempt to give permanence to the temporary.

M.P., 249

Disbelief

Atheism, nine times out of ten, is born from the womb of a bad conscience. Disbelief is born of sin, not of reason.

P.R., 27

Discipline

Taking away wives from husbands by force does not make them chaste, any more than confiscating productive property makes men devoid of the passion of greed. It is voluntary discipline the world needs and not an imposed discipline.

F.G., 231

There is nothing that develops character so much as a pat on the back, provided it is given often enough, hard enough, and low enough.

O.B., 206

Discussion

. . . discussion is also a most excellent means to avoid *decision*.

M.P., 20

Divinity

Divinity is so profound that it can be grasped only by the extremes of simplicity and wisdom. There is something in common between the wise and the simple, and that is humility.

E.G., 21–22

The modern world looks for Divinity and the solution of its ills in the superman of H. G. Wells, in the humanism of Irving Babbitt, in the sexualism of Sigmund Freud, in the cynicism of Bertrand Russell, in the naturalism of modern religion, in the book of the month, in the re-interpreted Christ, in the new morals, in the new psychology, in the new science—but in none of these inns is Divinity to be found. As it was not in the inn in the first century, so it shall not be found in the inn of the twentieth century, for what is true of the first day is true of our own: Divinity is always where you least expect to find it.

H.C., 7–8

Divorce

The alarming increase of divorces in our land and the consequent break-up of family life is due principally to the loss of love for the ideal in womanhood. Marriage has become identified with pleasure, not with love. Once the pleasure ceases, love ceases. The woman is loved not for what she is in herself but for what she is to others. The tragedy of such a state is not only what it does for woman, but also what it does for man.

S.V., 51

Whenever the laws and the customs of a country permit an arrangement whereby a woman can be discarded because she has dishpan hands, she becomes the slave, not of the dishpans, but of man.

T.M., 54

No person in all the world is made happier by the breaking of a pledged love.

T.M., 284

Divorce is inconstancy, infidelity, temporality, the very fragmentation of the heart.

W.L., 131

Doctorate (Modern)

Theses for the Ph.D. are so specialized as to give no knowledge to the general public, little to the department, and practically none to the students who wrote them.

D.L., 139

Dogmas

Indifference to truth was the principal dogma of individualism. Submission to a creed as the State understands it, is the principal dogma of the new Totalitarianism.

C.C., 175

. . . the Church holds that it is impossible to have a religion without dogmas. To say that one must have a religion without a dogma is to assert a dogma, and a dogma that needs tremendously more justification than any dogma of the Church. What is a dogma? A dogma is an idea, and in this sense a man without a dogma may be said to be a man without an idea. Dogmas there must be, just as long as there is sound thinking.

M.T., 143

The religious problem is not whether religion shall be free from dogmas or not, because, by the mere fact that a man thinks, he creates dogmas. The real problem is which dogmas are we going to accept, those of hearsay, private wish, or the funded intelligence of an august line of philosophers, saints, and mystics. For the life of me, I cannot see why any one should accept the authority of the Book of Darwin, and not accept the authority of the Book of Isaias; nor how any one can accept the authority of the latest psychological theory emanating from Vienna, and not accept the authority of twenty centuries of Christian tradition; nor how any one can accept the authority of H. G. Wells, and not accept the authority of Jesus Christ!

M.T., 145

Doing

It is typically American to feel that we are not doing anything unless we are doing something *big*.

S.W., 31

Drunkards versus Alcoholics

. . . if one becomes enslaved by alcohol and is poor, one is called a drunkard. If one becomes enslaved by alcohol and is rich, one becomes an alcoholic. The drunks go to jails; the alcoholics go to psychiatrists. There are few alcoholics on the Bowery; there are few drunkards on Park Avenue.

L.5, 74

Duty

It matters very little what we are doing; what does matter is that we are doing our duty. Sometimes the most humble occupations prepare for the greatest vocations. Society is built up from below.

C.I., 7

Duty must always take precedence over pleasure; recreation is the reward of work, not a preparation for it and therefore must always be earned.

D.L., 30

E

Easter (Modern)

Modernized, the Easter message means that God recycles human garbage. He can turn prostitutes like Magdalen into disciples, broken reeds like Simon Peter into rocks, and political-minded Simon Zealots into martyrs for the faith. *God is the God of the Second Chance.*

M.P., 126

Economic Determinism

Those who believe in an ethical order independent of economics can condemn exploitation, but the materialism of Communism cannot do it without repudiating the whole system. They have no right to use the words "right" and "wrong," but only "private" and "social." If everything is economically determined, right and wrong, truth and error have no existence, for they do not fit in an economic category.

L.I, 66

Economics

. . . the basic problem of the economic world is a spiritual one: what is the nature of man? Tell me what you believe about a man, and I will tell you your economics.

C.C., 75

Economics (False)

. . . false economics . . . says that the primary end of business is not consumption, but production. Start with this principle and it follows then that the purpose of a machine is not to supply human needs, but to make profit for its owner. The price then becomes more important than the *man* who pays the price. It is then only a step to say that the produce of God's bountiful land may be destroyed in the midst of starvation for the sake of an economic price. Man becomes subordinate to economics, instead of economics to man, and this means a degradation and impoverishment of human dignity.

P., 33

Eden

Economic conditions in the Garden of Paradise were excellent, but the first Red got in.

L.2, 104

Educated

If the frustrated soul is educated, it has a smattering of uncorrelated bits of information with no unifying philosophy. Then the frustrated soul may say to itself: "I sometimes think there are two of me—a living soul and a Ph.D."

P.S., 7

Education

It is a great fallacy for parents to believe that the education of their children depends on the school. The school is not the primary educator, but the secondary; its authority to teach the children is delegated by the parents, the right inherent in the father and the mother. Nor is the school ever a substitute for the parents.

D.L., 88

Every D.D. ought to be a saint; every Ph.D. ought to be as good as Plato or Socrates but, as a matter of fact, there are more saints among the non-D.D.s, and more good moral pagans among the non-Ph.D.s.

D.L., 100

In the definition of education it was observed that the purpose of education is to enter into contact not merely with environment but with the *totality* of environment, with an end to explaining the purpose of life. But the purpose of life cannot be understood without God, nor can any one enter into contact with the whole of environment unless he enters into relationship with God, in Whom we live and move and have our being.

O.E., 271

A man may know all we teach him and still be a bad man; the intelligentsia are not necessarily the saints. The ignorant are not necessarily devils.

P.W., 74

Unless a man's will has a purpose and it is a good one, education will do nothing for him except to fortify his own egotism.

P.W., 74

We are in a condition of society where the school has replaced the Church in education, and we are coming to a condition where the State will replace the school. Such is always the logic of history; when the family surrenders its rights, the State assumes them as its own. In order to avoid that condition, the new order must integrate in some way religion to education.

P.W., 138–139

The prime purpose of education is the making of a man, and it is impossible to make a man without giving him the purpose of being a man.

P.W., 159

An educator was once asked by a mother of a child of five years of age, at what age she should begin educating her child. His answer was that "it is already five years too late."

W.I., 14

Education (Modern)

Modern education makes no distinction between error and sin; it teaches that what we call evil is only an intellectual error.

G.C., 10

Students, instead of being given a very definite philosophy of life which they can explore all their days after they get their A.B. and their Ph.D., are given a point of view, a fad, a fancy, a theory which in ten or twenty years is antiquated.

L.2, 161

Never before has there been so much education and never before so little coming to the knowledge of the truth. We forget that ignorance is better than error.

S.W., 20

Educator (Progressive)

Our so-called liberal and progressive educators who denied the reality of guilt, did not, as they promised, relieve man from the shackles of "medieval morality"; but they did relieve the person of his responsibility and therefore of his freedom.

G.C., 18

If a little boy loses his temper and insults his father, he is not told that he is at fault; our progressive educators would not warp his mind by speaking of wrong—they blame it on his naughty ductless glands. Today nobody is wrong; they are anti-social or have bad tonsils.

W.W., 27

Ego

Hell is the ego affirmed in time, in isolation and in eternity in conflict with other egos who are constantly negating our ego.

D.L., 16

Egotism

Children are basically egotistic; that is one of the reasons why they hate to be laughed at. Extreme sensitiveness characterizes their every move. The adult who has never grown up to be humble is serious about even his failings.

L.4, 38

Egotism is . . . behind those who begin work and never finish it. They have dozens of books that are begun but never published; the reason is because they oscillate between ambition on the one hand and fear of criticism on the other. The dread that anyone should pronounce their work imperfect prevents them from working.

L.4, 57

Egotist

Nothing in nature is complete within itself; everything looks to something outside and beyond self except the egotist.

D.L., 119

The egotist reacts to every situation so as to make himself the leader of the parade. A very pompous bishop was once described by a group of the junior clergy as a "one-man procession."

G.T., 90

The egotist, standing alone in his self-imagined greatness, lives in a world of lie, because the truth about himself would puncture his self-inflation.

W.I., 119

Einstein, Albert

Einstein is mysterious; that is why the world likes his religion. The human mind likes mystery for the simple reason that it is meant for the mysterious infinite. But here the modern mind falls into a queer inconsistency. On the one hand, it refuses to accept anything beyond reason or without proof and declares that henceforth religion must be free from dogmas and mysteries. On the other hand, it accepts the dogmas of Einstein—every scientific statement is a dogma—and makes a religion out of them because they are mysterious. That brings up the question why the world should accept the mysteries of Einstein rather than the mysteries of Christ.

O.E., 260

Enemies

Divorce, infidelity, planned un-parenthood, invalid marriages are so many travesties and heresies against love—and whatever is the enemy of love is the enemy of life and happiness.

L.H., 69

Envy

The envious never know that their criticism of others is vicarious self-criticism. The man who accuses another of infidelity, jealousy or pride is generally guilty of those sins himself. Thus he projects to others his own faults and is judged in his judgment of others.

L.A., 83

If envy is on the increase today, as it undoubtedly is, it is because of the surrender of the belief of a future life and righteous Divine Justice. If this life is all, they think they should have all. From that point on, envy of others becomes their rule of life.

V.V., 17

Equality

The French Revolution made all men equal before the law; the Communist revolution makes all equal before the dictator.

F.G., 212

In vain will the world seek for equality until it has seen men through the eyes of faith. Faith teaches that all men, however poor, or ignorant, or crippled, however maimed, ugly, or degraded they may be, all bear within themselves the image of God, and have been bought by the precious blood of Jesus Christ. As this truth is forgotten, men are valued only because of what they can *do,* not because of what they *are.*

P.R., 195–196

Eros

But today the *eros* has become the erotic, which means one drinks the water, destroys the vessel—the pleasure enjoyed, the person ignored. The ego projects itself into another, pretends that it is worshiping the other when actually it is only idolizing its ego in the other person. The partner, then, is something only functional.

F.D., 84

Eroticism

The one universal phenomenon that eroticism seeks to conceal, namely death, is the one thing in common now between atheism and authentic Christianity. When death, as repentance, is suppressed in the Church, it breaks out in the Death of God in atheism.

M.P., 164

Escape

Modern man is not active; he is passive, in the sense that he is acted upon by forces which rush him to his own destruction. He is concerned only with the process and not with the product. That is why beatniks and alienated youth and bored writers of the rat race have a hatred both for the conventional, which refers to the past, and also for the future, which frightens them because of the absurdity of their lives. They think that by cutting off both the roots and the fruit that they avoid any commitment or responsibility. They avoid falling in love, for that means involvement for tomorrow; love affairs are for the moment. This makes them bizarre, deviants, the oddballs, and always rebels; but while strong in hates and negations, they are weak in lasting loves and affirmations. Life is a process, not a program, and one must be angry with it, because one is angry with oneself.

F.D., 13

Escapist

The escapists who call religion a crutch are like the blind who call those who see visionaries.

D.L., 120

By denying guilt they show that they are cowards; by denying any perfection outside themselves, they become snobs.

P.S., 180

Eternity

Eternity is without succession, a simultaneous possession of all joys. To those who live toward Eternity, it really is not something at the end; it is that which influences every moment of the "now."

F.D., 18

Ethics

Even Freud has admitted that from a medical point of view the unscrupulous method of satisfying every instinct may make the patient worse. Ethics is the very essence of sound medical treatment.

W.H., 138

Ethnic Sensitivity

A generation ago, the Irish, the Germans, and the Jews loved to have stories told about them; today, they regard such stories as an insult.

L.4, 38

Eucharist

. . . contrast the triple superiority of the Eucharistic over the Communistic Philosophy of Life. The Eucharist alone recognizes (1) the value of a man, which Communism despises; (2) the Eucharist emphasizes the primacy of brotherhood over equality which Communism falsely exalts, and (3) the Eucharist makes sacrifice and not class struggle the inspiration of battle.

C.C., 103

The faith in the Eucharist is the remedy for mental degeneration. Materialism is a foundation for a philosophy, but it is not the final philosophy of life. Spiritual truths are its complement, and faith gives the vision for these. Because the Eucharist demands faith of the right kind it is the proper therapeutic for bad thinking.

L.L., 77

Eugenics

The sterilization of the unfit, for example, is one form of the philosophy that maintains society's right to mutilate the integrity of human life. Eugenics, too, implies that society has a better right to choose the bride than the bridegroom has; birth-control propagandists and Malthus-minded groups maintain that ushering more children into the world than a society can assimilate is a form of bootlegging and is therefore unethical.

O.E., 245

The barbarism of the new era will not be like that of the Huns of old; it will be technical, scientific, secular, and propagandized. It will come not from without, but from within, for barbarism is not *outside* us; it is *underneath* us. Older civilizations were destroyed by imported barbarism; modern civilization breeds its own.

S.P., 110

The first direct, human limitation of infant life in the history of Christianity took place in the village of Bethlehem through an Infant-Controller whose name was Herod. The prevention of infant life was simultaneously an attack upon Divinity in the person of God made man, Jesus Christ, our Lord. No one strikes at birth who does not simultaneously strike at God, for birth is earth's reflection of the Son's eternal generation.

T.M., 218

Euthanasia

Merciful killing is a contradiction.

L.2, 36

In 1936, Hitler introduced the idea of merciless killing under the soothing but lying title of "Charitable Foundation for Institutional Care." The basic principle was that those who could not be of benefit to society should be killed. Up to the outbreak of the war, 275,000 people were put to death. Once the door was opened for destroying the sanctity of a single personality, there was nothing to stop slaughter.

L.2, 37

When Hitler called it "merciful," he did not define those to whom mercy was to be extended, unless it be the state. But once the idea is introduced that one may take the life of a person because he is not useful to the state, then it will not be long before we are taking his life because his ideas are not the same as those of the state.

L.2, 37

Evil

Evil may have its hour, but God will have His day.

E.I., 35

Men think that evil must come in the disguise of a germ, or a bomb, or a raid, or an explosion, or a train wreck, or a bank failure, forgetful that the greatest grief can come to man under the disguise of human ideals.

G.C., 9

Because the world assumes that evil is wholly external or social, it falsely believes that its remedy lies in the domain of politics and economics since they deal with the externals or with what a man *has* rather than what he *is*.

G.C., 16

The possibility, not the necessity, of moral evil, of wars and social injustices which follow them, is the price we have to pay for the greatest good we possess—the gift of freedom. God could, of course, at any moment stop a war, but only at a terrible cost—the destruction of human freedom.

L.A., 34–35

. . . the world is too often dedicated to explaining evil away instead of having it pardoned and forgiven.

L.4, 236

The possibility of evil is in some way bound up with the freedom of man. Since man was free to love, he was free to hate; since he was free to obey, he was free to rebel; since he was free enough to be praised for his goodness, he was free enough to be blamed for his badness.

M.U., 28

Evil in order to be attractive must at least wear the guise of goodness. Hell has to be gilded with gold of paradise, or men would never want its evil. If evil were always called by its right name, it would lose much of its appeal.

T.M., 23

Evil and Death

Once evil has come into the world, death is seen as a kind of blessing, for if there was no death, evil could go on forever. That is why God stationed an angel with a flaming sword at the Gate of Paradise, lest fallen man, eating of the tree of immortality, should immortalize his evil. But, because of death, evil cannot carry on its wickedness indefinitely.

P.S., 200

Evil (Experience of)

If you know evil by experience, are you wiser because of it? Have you not despised that very evil and are you not the more tragic for having experienced it?

S.W., 17

Example

Whenever a person sets out to give "good example," he generally does not give it.

W.I., 67

Excuses

. . . there is no field in which more excuses are given than in the realm of the spiritual and the moral. Any excuse is better than none for the acceptance of the word of God, which demands the pricking of the balloon of pride, and the surrender of the illegitimate revels of the flesh. That is why there has to be a Day of Judgment to send the excuses to Hell and the reasons to Heaven.

G.T., 89

Excuses and Reason

A reason is something we give before a conclusion is reached; an excuse is something we give for not following out the conclusion. Reasons generally are sincere; excuses generally are a rationalization of conduct. A reason is a reality; an excuse is an invention, or at least a weak reason.

G.T., 88

Existentialism

Stoicism prepared men for social nihilism, the decay of civilization; Existentialism bids men accept an inner nihilism, the decay of the human personality which has abandoned God. Existentialist philosophers do, at least, see clearly when they ask men to choose between the two supreme alternatives: God or nothing.

W.H., 180

Existentialist

The existentialist dies for his own sake, and the Christian dies for Christ's sake. One is centered in self-consciousness, and the other is centered in Other-consciousness.

F.D., 63

Externals

Outer truths had such primacy that Christ was abandoned. As the Church drops certain practices and ideals, the world picks them up and secularizes them. As the rosary is dropped, hippies put them around their necks; as nuns drop the long habits, girls put on maxi-coats; as mysticism is forgotten, youths go in for psychedelic experiences; as Christ is dropped, the theater restores Him as superstar.

M.P., 21

F

Facts

It is one thing to observe facts, another thing to interpret them. Facts as facts mean nothing; experience as experience means nothing. A cat walking through a laboratory sees the test-tubes and retorts just as well as the scientist—in fact sees them better in the dark. But the cat can make no conclusions concerning the facts, simply because it lacks the power of reason. It is reasoning on experience, then, that makes interpretation, and therefore I say that we are no better equipped to-day to interpret facts than the ancients were; we have only better facts to interpret.

O.E., 158

Fad

It is positively amazing the amount of ignorance that can be accumulated in the form of useless facts and passing theories, sociological moods and philosophical fancies.

L.2, 162

It is difficult for our generation to believe that Herbert Spencer was once as widely talked about as Freud is today, but who today ever reads Herbert Spencer?

L.4, 18

Faddist

Some change their philosophy of life with every book they read: one book sells them on Freud, the next on Marx; materialists one year, idealists the next; cynics for another period, and liberals for still another. They have their quivers full of arrows, but no fixed target.

L.I, 2

Failure

We can do worse than fail; we can succeed and be proud of our success and burn incense to our nets and despise those who fail and forget the Hand which both gives and withholds.

D.L., 31

Faith

As a scientist can reveal to me truths which are beyond my reason, so God can reveal to me truths beyond the power of my intelligence. Since I know Him to be One Who neither deceives nor can be deceived, I accept His revelation in faith.

G.T., 110

Faith is related not to self-assurance but to God; not to an event, but to truth. In fact, there is often the greatest faith when there is the least prosperity.

O.B., 17

Faith is not believing that something will happen, nor is it the acceptance of what is contrary to reason, nor is it an intellectual recognition which a man might give to something he does not understand or which his reason cannot prove, e.g., relativity. Faith is the acceptance of a truth on the authority of God revealing.

P.R., 184

The torch of Faith has been given to us not to delight our eyes but to enkindle the torches of our fellow men. Unless we burn and are on fire for the Divine Cause a glacial invasion will sweep the earth which will be the end, for "The Son of men, when he cometh, shall he find, think you, faith on earth?"

R.S., 71

What was the faith . . . that justified Abraham, who was the father of the Jews? It was the faith in the Messias, or the Christ Who was to come. There is no salutary faith except in Christ. The Jews believed in the Christ Who *was to come;* we believe in Christ Who *has come.* The times have changed, but the reality of faith has not changed. There is only one faith. The faith that saves all men, making them pass from carnal generation to spiritual birth.

T.A., 17

Fall of Man

This permanent wound in human nature cannot be explained away by biological evolution, as we tried to do a few years ago, because its essence is not the will to survive but pride which biology cannot touch.

P.W., 89

Family

Home life is the God-appointed training ground of human character, for from the home life of the child springs the maturity of manhood, either for good or for evil.

O.B., 170

The two most evident symptoms of the breakdown of the family are: divorce and voluntary or deliberate sterility, *i.e.* broken contracts and frustrated loves. Divorce destroys the stability of the family; voluntary sterility destroys its continuity. Divorce makes the right of living souls hang up the caprice of the senses and the terminable pact of selfish fancy; while voluntary sterility makes a covenant with death, extracting from love its most ephemeral gift while disclaiming all its responsibilities.

P.W., 120

If the bringing of children into the world is today an economic burden, it is because the social system is inadequate; and not because God's law is wrong. Therefore the State should remove the causes of that burden. The human must not be limited and controlled to fit the economic, but the economic must be expanded to fit the human.

P.W., 123

The State exists for the family, the family does not exist for the State.

S.P., 77

Family (Decline of)

No country better illustrates this than Russia. In the first flush of its atheistic Marxian Socialism, it denied the necessity of marriage, established abortion centers, ridiculed fidelity and chastity as a "bourgeois virtue," compared lust and adultery to drinking a glass of water, after which you could forget the glass in one instance, and the person in the other; introduced postcard divorces, which required only that you send a notice that you were no longer living with a certain party, and all obligations thereby ceased.

P.W., 131

Famine

Today, there is a famine for divine certainty and guidance among those who spent the capital of their belief in Sacred Scripture; there is a famine for a helping hand more kindly than the human among those who spent belief in His Divinity; there is a famine for perfect life, truth, and love, among those who spent belief in the Trinity. Everywhere there is a famine for faith among those who doubt, a famine for God among those who substituted illusions for majestic faiths, and a famine for love amongst those who war. Everywhere there is a feeling of emptiness like that which follows a fever or an unhappy love affair.

P., 16

Fascism

If Fascism means, as it does, the supremacy of the State or nation over the individual, with consequent suppression of rights or liberties, then the Church is anti-Fascist, as the Encyclical against Fascism so well proves. If by Fascism is meant anti-Communism and dislike of a system which suppresses the liberties, then the Church is Fascist, but so is every American who loves the democratic way of life more than the totalitarian.

C.P., 34

"Fascism" is never defined. It often means every one who is anti-Communistic; sometimes it means one who believes in God, or authority, or religion. As a matter of fact, we do not know what Fascism is; it is the subjection of the person to the State, as Nazism is the subjection of the person to the race, and as Communism is the subjection of the person to the class. But that is too clear cut to satisfy the muddle-minded. They want to keep it undefined, so as to beat down with a sneer any one who refuses to accept their political outlook.

S.P., 66

Fashion

The paradox of fashion is that everybody is trying at the same time to be like and to be unlike everyone else. The higher classes need not necessarily be aristocratic or noble or wealthy; they can simply be the creators of a new style.

L.5, 233

Fear

We fear because our false freedom and license and apostasy from God has caught up with us, as it did with the Prodigal.

G.C., 82

Feeling (Age of)

The reason why chastity is on the decline is that we live in a sensate culture. In the Middle Ages, there was an Age of Faith, then came the Age of Reason in the eighteenth century; now we are living in the Age of Feeling.

A., 203

Fifth Column

The university professor and the newspaper editor who ridicule the Divine in order to purge it from the hearts, or the radio director who eliminates all prayers and substitutes antireligious poems: these are Satan's fifth column. Here is not just a refusal to acknowledge Goodness, but a pretense that Goodness is badness, or as Nietzsche said: "Evil, be thou my good."

W.L., 194

Flattery

The amount of flattery one spreads on another depends on either how much one wishes to exalt his own ego, or how much one wishes to deceive the ego of the hearer.

W.I., 85

Rare are those who use such restraint in flattery in order to delude others into asking them to "say that again." A Bishop who was just consecrated was laughingly told, "From now on you will never hear the truth again."

W.I., 85

Football (College)

I heard of a college that was planning to have three football teams: one for offense, the other for defense, and the third to attend classes.

T.T., 142

Footnotes

It is easy to write a book with footnotes, because everything you do not understand or do not grasp thoroughly you put down at the bottom of the page, so that someone else can look it up.

L.2, 64

Forgiveness

The forgiveness of God is one thing, but the proof that we want that forgiveness is the energy we expend to make amends for the wrong.

D.L., 106–107

The Church is always willing to take the erring back into the treasury of her souls, but never the errors into the treasury of her wisdom.

M.P., 134

Fortitude

Fortitude may be defined as that virtue which enables us to face undismayed and fearlessly the difficulties and dangers which stand in the way of duty and goodness. It stands midway between foolhardiness, which rushes into danger heedlessly, and cowardice, which flees from it recreantly.

S.V., 13–14

Free Will

One will never find a professor who denies freedom of the will who does not also have something in his life for which he wishes to shake off responsibility. He disowns the evil by disowning that which made evil possible, namely, free will.

W.L., 20

Freedom

Freedom is the power to do what we *ought*. A man *can* do many things, e.g., shoot his wife, steal his neighbor's cabbage, or punch his competitor's nose. But he *ought* not do these things, because all his rights involve corresponding duties. The power to act a certain way is not the right to act any way.

F.G., 184

There is nothing the modern man prizes more than freedom, but does he realize that his denial of sin is the denial of freedom? Does not freedom imply choice? Does not choice imply alternatives of good and evil?

G.C., 17

Men talk most about freedom when they are losing it, as they talk most about health when they are sick.

G.C., 18

Freedom is not an heirloom, but a life. Once received, it does not continue to exist without effort, like an old painting. As life must be nourished, defended, and preserved; so freedom must be repurchased in each generation.

L.C., 275

Freedom is not so much a birthright, as it is an achievement. We are born with freedom of choice, but the way we use our choices makes us slaves or free men. Inner freedom of this kind is the last thing a man attains, and it is what St. Paul calls the "glorious liberty of the children of God."

L.H., 89

Morality implies responsibility and duty, but these can exist only on condition of freedom. Stones have no morals, because they are not free. We do not praise iron because it becomes heated by fire, nor do we condemn ice because it is melted by heat. Praise and blame can be bestowed only on those who are masters of their own will.

M.U., 27

Freedom, if we only knew it, is within the law of our nature, not outside it. Try to be so progressive and broadminded as to draw a giraffe with a short neck, or a triangle with four sides, and see where you end!

P.R., 47

The State must *guarantee* the social security of its citizens, but it must not *supply* that security. Freedom from want must not be purchased by freedom from freedom, in which a Bureaucratic State becomes the world's caterer.

S.P., 55

Freedom is ours to give away; we are free to choose our servitudes.

S.W., 94

Once God gives freedom, He never takes it back; that is why hell is eternal. Hell is the guarantee of human freedom, a place in which man with a clenched fist may thrust forever in the sight of God his *Non Serviam*.

T.T., 138

Freedom and Law

. . . freedom is conditioned upon obedience to law. There is no such thing as freedom *from* law; there is only freedom *within* law, whether that law be scientific, natural, human, or divine.

F.G., 31

Freedom (Liberal)

"Freedom is the right to do whatever I *please.*" This is the liberal doctrine of freedom, which reduces freedom to a physical, rather than to a moral, power.

W.L., 19

Freedom (Modern)

Freedom became synonymous with doing whatever you pleased, whether it was good or evil, or believing whatever you pleased whether it was true or false. The result was that freedom degenerated into a form of "selfishness," expressed itself in such slogans as "be yourself," frowned upon all forms of restraint and sacrifice as contrary to the individual libido, and ended in what might be called the exaltation and glorification of the ego.

P.W., 48

Freud, Sigmund

. . . the popularity of Freud is due to the fact that he made it possible for people to talk about sex under the guise of science.

P.S., 137

Freud and Marx

Two thinkers have made the thought of our times: Freud and Marx. Both were excavators. Both dug below the accepted maxims of humanity and unearthed ore: some would say for the weal of humanity, others for its woe. Freud burrowed below the consciousness into the subconscious or id. Marx quarried beneath the bourgeois sanity to the depths of the masses. When their profound ideas escaped the Vienna laboratory and the British Museum, they became popularized on the one hand as "self-expression" or the danger of repression, and on the other, "communism." The primacy of pleasure, the rejection of discipline and self-control, and sex license, became the pamphleteers' expression of Freud, whether he avowed these ideas or not. Revolution, socialism and *Mama*-ism became the heritage of the author of *Das Kapital* . . . Marx—Marcuse—Mao.

M.P., 13

Friendship

Nothing has so much contributed to the debasement of human relationships as the idea that friends are won by flattery.

T.M., 67

When persons are taken for granted, then is lost all the sensitiveness and delicacy which is the essential condition of friendship and joy.

T.M., 97

The best friends are those who know how to keep the same silences.

W.I., 148

Fundamentalism

Fundamentalism assumes that the Bible is fundamental. Catholicism retorts . . . that the Bible is not a book but a collection of books, and hence the question more fundamental than Fundamentalism is: Who gathered the books together, and declared that they would constitute a Bible, and be regarded as the revealed Word of God? To answer this question is to get to a body beyond a book, namely, a Church with a spirit; for Pentecost was not the descent of books on the heads of the Apostles but the descent of tongues. From that day on it was to be a tongue and a voice, and not a book, that would be fundamental in religion.

O.E., 78

"Funny Inside Feeling"

Rationalism, after becoming atheistic, became sentimental or emotional. Then were born the philosophies of "individual or religious experience": "I feel it in here." They substituted the stomach for the head. Later individual emotion became social or collective emotion. Reason or feeling, it was said, is not in man; it is in totality. Truth is correspondence with the whole. Such is the irrationality of Totalitarianism.

D.D., 2

G

Game Shows

Information and quiz programs have indoctrinated us into believing that the man who knows the colors of the three beards mentioned in Hamlet is wise; or who can tell what four novelists of the Victorian era wrote about oysters on the half-shell, is wise; and that if we do not know similar patches of information, we ought to dissolve into an emotional crumble.

G.W., 45

Gangsterism

One wonders how a man as intelligent as Lenin and so kind to his wife and others, could be politically so cruel. The answer is the ideology of Marx. When a gangster is arrested for cutting a rival into bits and drowning him in a sack in the river, the gangster's wife is always quoted as saying: "But Bozo was always so good and gentle and kind." Yes, in his home relations, but outside his home his philosophy of life was "gangsterism."

L.5, 19

Garbage

Ecological garbage is only the outward sign of moral garbage piled up in the hearts of men.

M.P., 57

Generosity

True generosity never looks to reciprocity; it gives neither because it expects a gift in return, nor because there is a duty or obligation to give. Charity lies beyond obligation; its essence is the "adorable extra." Its reward is in the joy of giving.

L.A., 111

Genius

It has been said that some of the great geniuses of the past never read half as much as the mediocre geniuses today, but what they read they understood and incorporated into a deeper dimension of knowledge.

W.I., 108

Gentlemen

The gentleman is the one who is modest and retiring, who waits first on the others and thinks of everyone but himself, and finds his chief happiness in making someone else happy; who, however poor

and humble anyone else may be, bears to them the open palm of
true nobility.

G.T., 123

Gentry (Learned)

The learned gentry of our modern world are unlearned because
they never have a doubt. They try to make everything clear, and
hence make everything mysterious. They forget that even nature
has a mystery; that there is something in this great cosmos of ours
which is just so terribly mysterious that we cannot "see" it, and that
is the sun. It makes us wink whether we like it or not, and yet, in
the light of that great natural mystery everything else in the world
becomes clear. So too in higher realms, it is in the light of such a
great supernatural mystery as the Incarnation that all things become clear, even the problem of evil.

O.E., 40

Gift

. . . those who seek applause for their gifts do not really give at all
—they buy. They are not surrendering—they are purchasing. They
are less impressed with the need of others than they are with the
heed that will be given to them. Their gift is a kind of a specula-
tion. They made an investment in publicity, and they look for their
adequate returns.

O.B., 150

Giving

It is one of the paradoxes of Christianity that the only things that
are really our own when we die is what we gave away in His name.
What we leave in our wills is snatched from us by death; but what

we give away is recorded by God to our eternal credit, for only our works follow us. It is not *what* is given that profits unto salvation; it is *why* it is given.

Gnosticism (Modern)

No greater lie was ever enunciated than the lie of Marx, repeated by Lenin and echoed by Stalin: "religion is the opium of the people," for to promise man a heaven if he lived virtuously was to satisfy reason more than to promise him "a pie in the sky," if he lived as a subversive revolutionist. It was all part of the modern agreement not to face the issue of death and hence the destiny of man.

D.D., 27

[The] sharp distinction between the natural and the supernatural order, between knowledge by reason and knowledge by infused faith, between the natural perfection of our nature and the supernatural perfection through grace, has been lost sight of in modern philosophy. The result has been that what really is a gift of God is now looked upon as natural to man, so that man, attributing to himself that Divine quality which makes him a partaker of the Divine nature, has divinized himself to just that extent.

G.I., 279

The superstition of Progress asserts itself in some such fashion as this in our class rooms, best-sellers and high-class journals: Man is naturally good and indefinitely perfectible, and thanks to great cosmic floods of evolution will be swept forward and forward until he becomes a kind of a god. Goodness increases with time, while evil and error decline. History represents the gradual but steady advance of man up the hill of the more abundant and happy life. No special institutions, no moral discipline, no Divine grace are necessary for the progress of man; for progress is automatic, due to the free play of natural forces and the operation of freedom in a world released from the superstition of religion. Because evil and sin are only vestigial remnants from the bestial past, evolution and science and education will finally eradicate them.

P.W., 42

It is not a very sweet pill for our civilized world to swallow, to realize that the false prophets of the last century who predicted an evolution of man into a god, and the necessary progress of humanity to a point where there would be no war or disease or death, were wrong, and we are now living in a century of war. It behooves humanity to admit that there is an evil tendency in man, and that this tendency when uncontrolled by morality and grace will devolve more rapidly than it will evolve.

W.I., 94

An age without faith is an age of superstition. Religious belief is so essential to the heart of man that once it is cast aside, some false form is called in to fill the void. Every epoch of materialism has been followed by an era of superstition in which minds believe everything as fanatics and quacks become shrines of worship and objects of adoration.

W.I., 186

The Goal

Those who lose sight of the goal often concentrate on mere motion and try to derive pleasure from it. They delight in turning the pages of a book, but never finish the story; they pick up brushes, but never finish a picture; they travel the seas, but know no ports. Their zest is not in the achievement of a destiny but rather in gyration and action for the mere sake of movement.

W.H., 163

Goals

People live ten, twenty, thirty, fifty years without a plan. No wonder they find their existence humdrum and tiresome. If they were farmers, they would probably plant wheat one week, root it up and plant barley the next; then dig up the barley and plant watermelon; then dig up the watermelon another week and plant oats. Fall comes around and they have no harvest; if they repeated that process for years, they could go crazy. It is the meaninglessness of life that makes it wearisome.

L.I, 2

God

God is a Spirit with whom the human spirit holds intercourse and the more profound that commerce, the greater the apostolic energy.

M.P., 145

In religions such as Buddhism, Confucianism, Hinduism and the like, man is the wooer and God the wooed; man the seeker, God the found. In the Judaic-Christian tradition, the role of man to God is that of mirror to light, echo to voice. What has revealed the love of God where we are concerned, is that He has sent His Only Begotten Son into the world so that we might have life through Him. That love resides not in our showing any love for God, but in His showing love for us first, when He sent out His Son to be atonement for our sins, and therefore our Saviour.

T.C., 7–8

God is perfect life because of perfect inner intellectual activity. There is no extrinsicism, no dependence, no necessary outgoing on the part of God.

W.L., 117

God as Becoming

. . . if God really is, then it is absurd to say that He is one thing in the fifteenth century and another in the twentieth. This is equivalent to saying that a thing is true at three o'clock but false at half-past four, and that two apples plus two apples make four apples on Monday but not on Friday. That all this should be called progress is a mystery, as if there could be progress without a fixed term.

R.G., 219–220

God and Social Action

Our Lord died for all men, and thus set up a new series of relationships with God. And from out of this new set of relationships, slum clearance and social justice and all the rest *follow*—but not otherwise.

S.C., 48

God (Fear of)

Fear of God is a very different thing: it is not a servile fear, such as a slave feels toward his tyrant, but a reverential fear, such as a child may have for a loving father.

W.H., 122

Gods

There are three possible kinds of God: the god of one's own ego, in which the atheist believes, and which is also the god of modern confusionism; the god of nature, of stone and gold and silver, which belonged to the old religions of idolatry; and the Supreme God, who made both man and nature, and redeemed them both upon the Cross.

Those who tell us that they deny the existence of God are merely substituting one god for another.

O.B., 29–30

Gods (False)

The enthusiasm for false gods cannot be drowned by an indifference to the true God. No secularized, non-religious theory of political freedom is strong enough to overcome them. A people who lack the strength of an ultimate conviction, cannot overcome their faith or their false absolute. The effective answer to a false religion is not indifference to all religion, but the practice of a true religion. Their totalitarian, false religion can be overcome only by a total true religion. If they have made a politics into a false religion, we shall have to see that religion has something to say about politics.

P.W., 168

Let us admit the fact: Before picking up stones to cast at the adulteresses abroad, we ought to turn the searchlight into our own consciences. How many of us who protest against the destruction of churches and synagogues abroad ever go into a church or synagogue? What is the use of the world overthrowing a Hitler or a Stalin if it keeps the spirit that breeds them? To oppose a nation justly as the enemy of God we must believe in God: we may not smash its idols and keep our own.

W.W., 9

Golf

The golfer, too, is full of pride who smashes his club and says, "That was a rotten shot." By that he means "This is really not my normal game." One golfer said, "I have not been on my normal game for thirty years."

L.1, 44

A wife cannot understand why a husband will delight in swinging a golf club all day and yet be unwilling to beat a carpet though seventy is par for a rug.

L.4, 55

There is sometimes a seriousness about golf, for the greatest crime that one can commit when another golfer is shooting is to whisper.

L.4, 55

Good

There is more happiness in rejoicing in the good of others, than in rejoicing in our own good.

W.H., 144

Goodness

There is much more goodness in most people than shows on the surface.

W.I., 110

Goodness of God

The Goodness of God means that God gives us what we *need* for our perfection, not what we *want* for our pleasure and sometimes for our destruction.

P.R., 24

Gospel Message

In contrast with modern prophets the message of Our Blessed Lord was not smart and sophisticated, but plain and simple. There is nowhere an attempt to impress His auditors either with His Omniscience or with their nescience. He is never complex. There is no trick of rhetoric, no appeal to the intelligentsia, no pomp of demonstration, no monotonous deserts of laws and precepts such as are found in Buddha or Mohammed.

E.G., 96

Gossip

We cannot gossip without either overrating ourselves or underrating our neighbors . . . and frequently we do both.

O.B., 28

Traditionally, all gossips are women; but men are often guilty of the same offense. They call it "judging."

W.H., 156

The readiness to believe evil about others is in a large part ammunition for a thousand scandals in our own hearts. But by finding black spots in others, they believe they distract attention from their own miserable state. The good conscience, on the contrary, finds good in others even when there is some discontent with self.

W.I., 55

Grace

What is true in the order of nature is true in the order of supernature or grace. Only those who use the graces they are given are given more.

D.L., 100

Grace is a participation in the nature and life of God.

H.C., 81

Grace makes man more than a "new creature," and infinitely higher than his former condition, than an animal would be if it spoke with the wisdom of Socrates. There is nothing in all creation like that gift by which God calls man a son, and man calls God "Father."

L.L., 106

Grace does not work like a penny in a slot machine. Grace will move you only when you want it to move you, and only when you let it move you. The supernatural order supposes the freedom of the natural order, but it does not destroy it.

P.R., 105

The less grace there is in the soul, the more ornament must be on the body.

P.S., 21

Curiously enough, it is a fear of how grace *will* change and improve them that keeps many souls away from God.

P.S., 227

The acceptance of grace is not a passive thing; it demands a surrender of something, even if it is only our pride.

P.S., 241

Gratitude

Gratitude is characteristic only of the humble. The egotistic are so impressed by their own importance that they take everything given them as if it were their due. They have no room in their hearts for recollection of the undeserved favors they received.

O.B., 325

Greatness

The really great things of the world are not always the immense things; great men are always little men in the sense that they are humble, as Cardinal Mercier was. They are so big they can always be seeming little, because it is only "seems." . . . Greatness is not in size. Little things are much more impressive. Man never stumbles over a cosmos, though he does stumble over a rug.

O.E., 22

Guilt

Guilt is not just the breaking of a love; it is the wounding of someone who is loved.

L.C., 125

One must always distinguish between an abnormal manifestation of guilt and guilt itself. For example, a person given to excessive washing of the hands is manifesting an abnormal sense of guilt, but this does not alter the fact that behind this particular complex there may be a very real reason for a sense of guilt. A denial of guilt is a denial of responsibility, and a denial of responsibility is a denial of freedom. Illustrating the attitude of those who insist on having rights but no duties, freedom but no responsibility, praise but no blame, is a cartoon in which a psychoanalyst is pictured telling a mother: "Yes, your boy is stubborn, cruel, perverted, a kleptomaniac, has criminal tendencies—but bad, no."

L.5, 250

Freud secularized the Sacrament of Penance by explaining guilt as a psychological state of a patient, who allowed the animal impulses of his *id* to be contravened by the super-ego of society. From that point on, what was once described as sin, is now not forgiven, but explained away.

M.P., 160–161

Only the innocent can grasp guilt thoroughly. We are infected by it and cannot understand it, as a patient with a high fever and delirium does not understand his illness as well as the physician.

M.P., 175

Some men delight in boasting of their atheism, then agnosticism, their perversities, but no conscience ever boasted of its guilt. Even in isolation, the sinner is ashamed.

P.S., 115

Guilt is guilt only when it is subjectively felt as one's own. If a man does not know within himself that he is harsh or spiteful or proud, he does not know himself.

P.S., 115

The fondness of the twentieth century for scandal is due to a great extent to its guilty conscience. By finding others' skirts stained with mud, some rejoice that their dusty and ragged ones are not so bad after all.

W.I., 39

H

Habit

The great advantage of habit is that it saves us a lot of attention, effort and brain work.

D.L., 46

Hair Shirt

There is not much need in the twentieth century of wearing hair shirts for sanctity, because there are enough people around us who take the place of hair shirts; we can sanctify our lives by bearing their boredom.

L.4, 208

Happiness

Every man is passionately fond of liberty, but there is one thing he craves even more, and without which existence and even liberty is painful, and that is happiness. It is one of the greatest of life's paradoxes that as much as man seeks to be free, he still wishes to be a slave: not a slave in the sense that his liberty is denied him, but in the sense that he yearns for something he can worship, something which will solicit his will, pull at his heartstrings, tempt his energies, and command his affections. He wants to be free to choose between the various kinds of happiness, but he does not want to be free from happiness. He wishes to be its slave.

E.G., 111

One of the greatest deceptions of today is the belief that leisure and money are the two essentials of happiness. The sad fact of life is that there are no more frustrated people on the face of the earth than those who have nothing to do and those who have too much money for their own good. Work never killed anybody, but worry has.

P.S., 23

Our happiest times are those in which we forget ourselves, usually in being kind to someone else. That tiny moment of self-abdication is an act of true humility: the man who loses himself finds himself and finds his happiness.

W.H., 21

Hatred

. . . hatred has become a more rapidly unifying bond among nations than love.

D.D., 8

Evil has no capital of its own, it is a parasite on goodness. Pure hatred draws its blood from contact with goodness; this makes hell begin on earth, but it does not make it end here.

L.C., 300

. . . what is hatred but love upside down?

M.W., 161

It is not hatred that is wrong; it is hating the wrong thing that is wrong. It is not anger that is wrong, it is being angry at the wrong thing that is wrong. Tell me your enemy and I will tell you what you are. Tell me your hatred and I will tell you your character.

V.V., 10

To Have

It was creation that introduced the verb "have." When there was only God, before the world was made, there was only one verb, and only one form of the verb—namely, the infinitive "to be"—to indicate the Supreme being of God. God *has* nothing, but because He is sheer being, He is infinitely rich. If God had anything, it would be a sign that He needed something external to Himself in order to perfect His being.

G.T., 141

Heaven

. . . it is the mystery of the Trinity which gives the answer to the quest for our happiness and the meaning of Heaven. Heaven is not a place where there is the mere vocal repetition of alleluias or the monotonous fingering of harps. Heaven is a place where we find the fullness of all the fine things we enjoy on this earth. Heaven is a place where we find in its plenitude those things which slake the thirst of hearts, satisfy the hunger of starving minds, and give rest to unrequited love. Heaven is the communion with perfect Life, perfect Truth, and perfect Love.

D.R., 36–37

Heaven and Hell

Heaven and Hell are the natural and inseparable results of acts good and bad in the supernatural order. This life is the springtime; judgment is the harvest.

L.L., 121

Heaven, Purgatory, Hell

Heaven is Love without Pain; Purgatory is Pain with Love; Hell is Pain without Love.

H.C., 83

Hedonist

. . . the man who lives only for his own impulses keeps very bad company.

W.H., 33

Hell

If there is any subject which is offensive to modern sentimentalists it is the subject of hell. Our generation clamors for what the poet has called "a soft dean, who never mentions hell to ears polite," and our unsouled age wants a Christianity watered so as to make the Gospel of Christ nothing more than a gentle doctrine of good will, a social program of economic betterment, and a mild scheme of progressive idealism.

H.C., 93

Why do souls go to Hell? In the last analysis, souls go to Hell for one great reason, and that is—they refuse to love. Love pardons everything except one thing—refusal to love.

L.L., 121

Hell is one of the eternal guarantees of human freedom, for it admits the right of a free man to cry out *non-serviam* through all eternity.

O.B., 161

The basic reason why moderns disbelieve in hell is because they really disbelieve in freedom and responsibility. To believe in hell is to assert that the consequences of good and bad acts are not indifferent.

P.R., 147

Hell is eternal suicide for hating love. Hell is the hatred of the God you love.

P.R., 153

Heresy

Every heresy in the history of the Church has been either a truth exaggerated to an excess, or diminished to a defect.

M.T., 90

Heresy (Modern)

Minds no longer object to the Church, because of the way they *think,* but because of the way they *live.* They no longer have difficulty with the Creed, but with her Commandments; they remain outside her saving waters, not because they cannot accept the doctrine of Three Persons in One God, but because they cannot accept the moral of two persons in one flesh; not because Infallibility is too complex, but because the veto on Birth Control is too hard; not because the Eucharist is too sublime, but because Penance is too exacting. Briefly, the heresy of our day is not the heresy of thought; it is the heresy of action.

C.C., 142–143

Hero

The heroes must be prepared for the mockery of the weak.

D.L., 120

It has been said that no man is a hero to his valet. It would be truer to say that no man is a hero to himself.

W.I., 50

Herod

The . . . revealing act of Herod is his treatment of John the Baptist. He had invited John the Baptist into his palace not to hear the truth of his preaching but to enjoy the thrill of his oratory. There are so many in the world that way: they do not want to be better; they want only to feel better. But John was not the type of preacher who toned down his Gospel to suit the paganism of his hearers. Because he condemned Herod's second marriage, he lost his head. Everyone in the world at one time loses his head, but it is better to lose one's head John's way in the defense of truth, rather than Herod's way, in wine and passion.

C.P., 47

Hierarchy of Life

There is hierarchy of life in the universe and the life of man is higher than any other life, not because he has nutritive powers like a plant, not because he has generative powers like a beast, but because he has thinking and willing powers like God. These constitute his greatest claim to life and in losing these he becomes like to a beast.

L.L., 24

Historic Tragedy

The great tragedy of history is not that men should fall, but that they should fail to rise to full realization of their vocation as children of God, in other words, that they should miss so much. All about us we see vast multitudes of men and women of refinement and culture, endowed with intelligence and possessed of every natural virtue and every now and then swept by noble emotions and ideals, but who are living second-rate, superficial, unimportant and morally insignificant lives, because they have never had their nature enkindled into flame by the Spirit of Christ.

M.B., 258

History

History attests that religion has not encroached upon the temporal sphere, but rather jealous temporal rulers have invaded the spiritual. Sometimes these rulers were kings and princes, even so-called "Catholic defenders of the faith." Today they are dictators.

C.P., 38

History is always passing judgment on the decisions of men, for history develops in the framework of Divine Justice and not outside it. The fall of Rome was a judgment on human pride; the Religious Revolution was a judgment on human sin; the French Revolution was a judgment on human avarice and selfishness.

D.D., 96

History is not just a record of different things that have happened to ancient peoples; it is also a record of the *same* things happening to new people. He who knows history will not be a prey to the theory of "automatic progress," nor will he be without a standard to judge the "commentator-mentality," which identifies the latest with the most important.

L.5, 276

The English never seem to remember history; the Irish never forget it; the Russians never admit it; the Japanese never make it; and the Americans never learn it.

L.2, 20

Hitler-Stalin Pact

. . . when Molotov signed the treaty with the Nazis, he said, "Our friendship has been sealed in blood," meaning, of course, in the blood of Poland.

L.4, 269

Holiness

Holiness is the last argument that can be used to win over erotic souls; but in days of the erotic, holiness is a scarce commodity.

M.P., 265

Holiness is like salt; its usefulness to others must begin with self. As only the wise man can impart wisdom to others, so only the saintly can communicate sanctity. A man can bring forth to others only those treasures which he already has in his own heart.

O.B., 58

To do God's Will until death, that is the inner heart of all holiness.

W.L., 223

Holocaust

Were the six million Jews incinerated by Hitler totally alien to an enduring Calvary? Dachau and Auschwitz really were the new minutes on the clock of Golgotha, the hands of which are ever turning. In them once more Christ is driven "outside the camp."

M.P., 101

Christianity challenged the belief that the worship men owed to Caesar was total and complete; it affirmed that man had a soul and hence was not obligated to the political in the totality of his being. But the emperors, in claiming divinity, sentenced hundreds of thousands of Christians to death, for there was only one lord to them, which was Caesar.

O.B., 270

Man's misuse of freedom became for God the occasion of offering Himself as a Holocaust of love, not to force men back to Him, for His hands and feet were nailed, but to entice them back by a revelation of greater love in which He laid down His life for His friends. Those who understand this victory of love over evil see that all the free choices of the world should be dedicated to the perfection of the soul in love. In seeing this, man comes to the understanding of what is the greatest freedom in all the world, namely, the freedom to be a saint.

T.T., 138–139

Holy Communion

In the marriage act, love is triune: wife gives self to husband and husband to self and out of that mutual self-giving is born the ecstasy of love. The spirit too must have its ecstasy. What the union of husband and wife is in the order of flesh, the union of the human and the Risen Christ is in Holy Communion.

M.P., 157

Holy Spirit

They who have not the Spirit call him "a great man," "a teacher," "a master"; but to see Him as the Lord of heaven and earth, as the Son of the Living God, comes only through the Holy Spirit.

P.N., 91

Homosexuality

A popular God-is-dead book in the United States argues that homosexuality will become normal in a humanistic society where there is no restriction of morals which come from religion. St. Paul declared homosexuality and atheism were related to one another as effect to cause.

F.D., 213

Hubris

Notice how often today authors will have their picture taken with their book in their left hand, the title in full view of the camera, so that the photograph may tell the story: "Look Ma! My Book!" Television commentators have books on their desks with the title toward the audience so that the audience may be impressed. No man who reads books at a desk ever has the titles turned away—but toward himself. Perhaps some day when there are diaphanous walls, the intelligentsia will keep the titles on their bookshelves turned toward the wall so their next door neighbor will know how smart they are.

W.I., 13

Human Condition

In virtue of man's dual nature, he is therefore a part of a whole, a citizen in the State, and yet possessed of rights independent of the State; a soldier in an army and yet a captain of himself; bound to the State and yet the State is bound to him; immanent in the social order, and yet transcendent to it. He is in the State—but not of it —an entity belonging to two worlds; a political animal, and a theological creature.

F.G., 140–141

On this human level man knows that he came from God and that to God he must return. Hence the universe is to be viewed sacramentally as a material thing to be used for the purpose of leading the good life.

L.A., 62

Human Rights

There are some jurists in our land who contend that the principle of the sacredness of human rights is merely an expression of 18th century philosophy, or a false 'totem,' or an assumption of the *Aufklärung* movement. They quite forget that though the Declaration of Independence gave an 18th century expression to these ideas, the truths themselves were nevertheless eternal. As long as man has been a creature endowed with an intelligence and will and made to the image and likeness of God, he has been the possessor of rights and freedom. Once God is denied as the Source of rights, the State sets itself up as an absolute.

W.W., 62

Humanae Vitae

The press and sometimes theologians said that the Holy Father should never have issued the letter because it *divided the Church.* Of course it divided the Church as Elijah divided those who had to choose either Baal or God; it divided the Church as the Lord divided it: "He that gathereth not with Me, scattereth.

M.P., 142

I believe that the *Humanae Vitae* is one of the great tests of the Church in our times. We live in days of moral laxity, where there is a shrinking from responsibility for rearing children and a love of carnal experience divorced from love of person. In that world where love and life are made discontinuous, Paul VI affirms the deep relatedness of one to the other. It was not an infallible decision; that would have too clearly separated sheep from goats; it was only a moral decision of the Chief Shepherd that the Vatican Council said the faithful should obey.

M.P., 142

Humanism

The human never long remains the Humanist, for either beast or angel he becomes, but not just man! If you came from the beast, you cannot leave the beast behind. But if you came from God then you can leave humanity behind and be a child of God! This is true Humanism, where man finds his center in his Source.

S.C., 20

Humanism (Secular)

Humanism has been defined as "the endeavor to keep the best spiritual values of religion while surrendering any theological interpretation of the universe." In its broadest sense it is an endeavor to have Christianity without Christ, godliness without God, and Christian hope without the promise of another life.

O.E., 215

Once the modern mind denied that man was a creature made in the image and likeness of God, it naturally fell into the error of saying that man was made in the image and likeness of the beast. . . . But, if man is not different from nature, then what value has man? If there is no specific difference between a man and a horse, then why not yoke man to the plow of Nazism or the tractor of Marxian Socialism, or make him an instrument of the State as the Fascist intelligentsia teach today.

P.W., 52

Humanist

Humanists of our day had their prototypes on Calvary on Good Friday. They were those whom Sacred Scripture calls the "passers-by"; a significant term indeed for it suggests those who never remain long enough with religion to know anything about it, those who think themselves wise because they have had a passing acquaintance with Christ.

S.C., 12

Humanity

Humanity is not like a fence of separate poles, strung together thanks to political and economic barbed wire or red tape; rather it is like a giant tree which has been growing for centuries. Its leaves fall off now and then, but they are replaced by others, while the roots become deeper, and one mysterious energy or sap continues to flow, uniting the trunk and branches.

F.D., 120

. . . is it not a strange paradox that men who most wildly disclaim against religion are those who wish to make a religion out of irreligious humanity? Humanity can never be the object of religion for the very reason that a self-centered humanity would be just as chilling as a self-centered individual. Furthermore, there is no such thing as humanity, practically speaking. There are only men; only Peters and Pauls, Marys and Anns.

L.L., 65

Humble

The humble person is embarrassed with praise because he knows that his voice, his talents or his power come to him from God.

D.L., 121

. . . there is no one in heaven who did not become humble.

O.B., 147

Humility

Humility is not self-contempt but the truth about ourselves coupled with a reverence for others; it is self-surrender to the highest goal.

D.L., 121

The salvation of modern man lies not in a pride of what he knows, but in a humility concerning how little he knows. His omniscience must give way to nescience; instead of feeling he knows everything, he must come closer to the truth that he really knows nothing.

G.W., 46

Humility in relation to love means thinking others better than ourselves. One advantage of this is that it gives us some examples to imitate. Pride, on the other hand, sometimes seeks first place that others may say, "Oh! What greatness!" Pride, too, can subtly take the *last* place that others may say, "What humility!"

L.I, 43

The humble man is not cast down by the censures or the slights of others. If he has unconsciously given occasion for them, he amends the faults; if he deserves them not, he treats them as trifles.

W.I., 120

The bitterest draught man can ever drink is the confession of his utter inadequacy. The world says that at this moment man is at his worst; actually he is at his best. Man is at his worst if he falls into despair; but he is at his best if humbled.

W.I., 173

Humility (New)

The modern man is humble, not with that old humility which made a man doubt his power, but with the new humility that makes a man doubt his humanity. The old humility was grounded on truth: man is what he really is. The new humility is grounded on insignificance: man is only a speck in the cosmos.

O.E., 15

Humor

No one has ever laughed at a pun who did not see in the one word a twofold meaning. To materialists this world is opaque like a curtain; nothing can be seen through it. A mountain is just a mountain, a sunset just a sunset; but to poets, artists, and saints, the world is transparent like a window pane—it tells of something beyond; for example, a mountain tells of the Power of God, the sunset of His Beauty, and the snowflake of His Purity.

T.A., 7

Hunger

Hunger is not just an *economic* problem; it is a *moral and spiritual* problem. It is a greater danger to the future of mankind than is atomic war.

F.D., 156

The whole world is dying of hunger—the Eastern world is dying of hunger of body; the Western world is dying of hunger of soul.

W.I., 70

Hypochondria

There are some people who make themselves mentally sick. Actually, there are cases on record, for example, of men saying . . . "If I had not been sick, I would have written one of the finest novels that has ever been produced," "If I had not been sick, I would have been a millionaire," etc. Such people induce sickness out of fear of being called upon to fulfill their boasts or out of fear of their weakness and ignorance being discovered.

L.I, 118

Hypocrite

There are others who like to see their neighbor criticized and their reputations ruined in order that they might have the feeling that they are not so evil in comparison. The vultures are always the first to smell the carrion.

D.L., 127

He picks up a stone to throw at an adulteress and forgets that he helped to make her one.

W.W., 21

I

Ideas

It is not the bad dictators who made the world bad; it is bad thinking. It is, therefore, in the realm of ideas that we will have to restore the world!

P.W., 5

Identity

The only ones who suffer from the problem of identity are those who have no goal, no destiny, no eternal shore. . . . How do we know our identity? By limits, by laws, by destinies, by God. Once the Good Friday-Easter Sunday syndrome is made the rule of life, then one sees that only the Christ-fettered are free.

M.P., 127

Ideologies and Man

According to the present ideology of Fascism, Communism, and Nazism, the individual man has no value except as a fraction of the whole. Each man is merely a quantitative addition to the totality like another brick in a house. The collectivity continues to exist when he is gone. It alone has "immortality"; he is the stick tossed into the collective bonfire to keep it blazing for another generation.

F.G., 137

Idleness

What costs nothing amounts to nothing. Nature gives man corn, but he must grind it; God gives man a will, but he must make right choices. As Goethe said: "An idle life is death anticipated."

D.L., 68

Physical idleness deteriorates the mind; spiritual idleness deteriorates the heart.

W.H., 59

Idol (Modern)

The idol of our century is not the saint, but the man who has won through to "the top."

W.H., 109

Ills

The ills of man can be reduced to three—*physical:* such as sickness and disease; *mental:* doubts, mental retardation, skepticism, atheism, etc.; *moral:* sin and guilt.

M.P., 52

Imagination

. . . all the poetry of love is a cry and a moan, and the more pure it is, the more it pleads; the more elevated it is above the earth, the more it laments. If a cry of joy interrupts this pleading, it is to celebrate the ravishing of an hour, and then to fall back into the immensity of desire. That is why our nature is fortified by the imagination which puts before us the thought of the beautiful, so that when earthly beauty has faded from our eyes, we might revive the ideal more beautifully still in our imagination.

H.C., 44

Imitation

Most people are followers, not leaders. In fact, the more rapid the methods of communication, the more numerous will be the imitators.

D.L., 96

Immaculate Conception

And it had to be that the Mother of God was sinless in order that we might more easily believe that she had flung before the face of

the world woman's greatest challenge to sin—the vow of virginity
—and kept it and made it bear divine fruit.

W.L., 58-59

Immortality

Death has unexpectedly become a phenomenon that not only the
person must face, but society or civilization itself. Those who denied personal immortality used to take refuge in collective immortality, saying that, although the individual perished, society would
be preserved. The atomic bomb has made collective immortality a
myth and restored personal immortality as the great problem of
our age.

W.L., 229

Incarnation

Love tends to become like the one loved; in fact, it even wishes to
become one with the one loved. God loved unworthy man. He
willed to become one with him, and that was the Incarnation.

D.R., 70

Independence (Declaration of)

All quarrels, disagreements, wars, strifes, and dissensions begin
with a false declaration of independence—independence from God
and independence from fellowman.

S.C., 56

Indifference

Indifference means the denial of the distinction between the true and the false, right and wrong. Confusing charity and tolerance, it gives an equal hearing, for example, to speech which advocates the freedom to murder and to speech which advocates the freedom to live. Indifference is never a stable condition, but passes into polarization.

M.W., 7

Individualism

Individualism had two consequences: *isolation* and *indifference*.

C.C., 168

Inferiority Complex

Most people really do not suffer from a sense of inferiority, but a sense of superiority.

L.2, 74

Influence

What we say is less important in the way of influence than what we do.

W.I., 68

The best influences in life are indeliberate, unconscious; when no one is watching, or when reaction to the good deed was never sought.

W.I., 68

Ingratitude

Ingratitude is always the note of the loafer, whether rich or poor.

F.D., 115

Innocence

"He that is without sin among you, let him cast the first stone." The implication is clear: innocence alone has the right to condemn. But innocence will always wish to take on the guilt of the other, to atone for his failings as if they were his own. Love recognizes the sin, but love also dies for it.

O.B., 29

Purity is never suspicious but looks for some ground for reposing trust.

W.I., 132

The instinctive reaction of good children to evil is not due to their rational immaturity, but to their maturity in innocence.

W.I., 132

The sensitiveness of innocence does not mean ignorance or "not having lived." Rather it is an awareness of what is good and true because one has avoided the false and the evil.

W.I., 132

Instincts

It is also argued that all of our instincts are right, and therefore should be obeyed. But it must not be forgotten that the instincts in man are subject to reason, and therefore are to be rationally and morally guided. A man has a hunting instinct just as a fox does, but it is not rational for husbands to hunt mothers-in-law.

G.T., 57

Intellect

Our intellects do not make the truth; they attain it: they discover it.

R.G., 293

Intelligentsia

. . . those who have been educated beyond their intelligence.

L.A., 41

The intellectual never loses that compassion for the multitude which characterized the Word Incarnate. The intelligentsia, on the contrary, live apart from tears and hunger, cancer and bereavements, poverty and ignorance. They lack the common touch. Only the cream of bookish learning and not the milk of human kindness flows through their veins.

P.N., 22

Intimacies

Love has three and only three intimacies: speech, vision, and touch. These three intimacies God has chosen to make His love intelligible to our poor hearts. God has spoken: He told us that He loves us: That is Revelation. God has been seen: That is the Incarnation. God has touched us by His grace: That is Redemption.

E.G., 156

Islam

If Moslemism [Islam] is a heresy, as Hilaire Belloc believes it to be, it is the only heresy that has never declined. Others have had a moment of vigor, then gone into doctrinal decay at the death of the leader, and finally evaporated in a vague social movement. Moslemism, on the contrary, has only had its first phase. There was never a time in which it declined, either in numbers, or in the devotion of its followers.

W.L., 171

Izvestia and *Pravda*

. . . it is well to remember that there are two important Moscow newspapers: one called *Pravda* and the other, *Izvestia*. One means *Truth* and the other, *News*. In Russia they say that "there is no News in the Truth and no Truth in the News."

L.2, 11

J

Jargon

There seems to be an insane dread of using moral terms, or even condemning anything on moral grounds. Psychological terms, the lingo of sociology, even medical terms such as "complexes" are invoked with an air of scientific certitude, but "bad" or "good," "right" or "wrong" seem to be scrupulously avoided. About the only time the word "good" is used is when the mother of a bad boy, a mother who completely neglected her husband and her children, is quoted in the press as saying of her son who has just committed murder, "He was a good boy."

O.B., 320

Jealousy

Jealousy, which has been instinctively inseparable from the beginnings of love, is a denial of promiscuity and an affirmation of unity. Jealousy is nature's vanguard to monogamy.

T.M., 159

Jealousy is the tribute which mediocrity pays to genius.

W.I., III

Jefferson and Lincoln

To Jefferson goes the credit of writing our Declaration of Independence. To Lincoln goes the credit of writing our Declaration of Dependence. Jefferson declared we were independent from tyrants; Lincoln added, we are dependent on God. The ethical complement to our Bill of Rights, he told us, is our Bill of Duties.

D.V., 44

Jesus Christ

Our blessed Lord began His public life on the Mount of Beatitudes, by preaching: "Blessed are the meek: for they shall possess the land." He finished His public life on the hill of Calvary by practicing that meekness: "Father, forgive them, for they know not what they do."

C.B., 3

He who later on called Himself "the Living Bread descended from Heaven" was born in Bethlehem—which in Hebrew means "house of bread." And He was laid in a manger—a place of food—as if to show us that as we have bread for our bodies, so He would be the Bread of our souls.

J.S., 8

One can sell Christ as Judas did, but one cannot buy Him.

L.2, 207

If He is not the Eternal Contemporary, He is not God.

P.R., 94

Jesus Christ and the State

Even though Christ Himself would not deliver us from the power of the Totalitarian State, as He did not deliver Himself, we must see His purpose in it all. Maybe His children are being persecuted by the world in order that they might withdraw themselves from the world. Maybe His most violent enemies may be doing His work negatively, for it could be the mission of totalitarianism to preside over the liquidation of a modern world that became indifferent to God and His moral laws.

C.P., 41

Jews

Few people on the face of the earth suffered as much in recent years as the Jews. Shall Christians despise them who through suffering have become more like our Master than they themselves become through their hate and criticism?

L.A., 126

The Jews will never crush anti-Semitism so long as they protest against intolerance only within their ranks, or within their press, and completely ignore the intolerance shown to Christians. And the same is true of Christians. Not until they both protest out of a common relationship, until the Jew defends the Christian and the Christian the Jew, will there be peace.

S.C., 56

Journalism

There seems to be an insane dread of using moral terms, or even condemning anything on moral grounds. . . . The conspiracy is to use any word at all except the one word which would take one into the field of ethics—on which every civilization is built.

D.L., 137–138

Journalism (Modern)

In journalism, the modern man wants controversy, not truth.

T.T., 132

Journalist

The journalist tells you what happens; the theologian not only why it happens, but also what matters.

P.W., I

Joy

Lightness of spirit is related to Redemption, for it lifts us out of precarious situations. As soon as a priest goes in for revolutionary tactics in politics he becomes boringly serious. This world is all there is, and therefore he takes political involvements without a grain of salt. One rarely sees a Commissar smile. Only those who are "in the world, not of it" can see events seriously and lightly. Joy is born by stradling two worlds—one the world of politics, the other of grace.

M.P., 238

Joy is not derived from the things we get or the people we meet; it is manufactured by the soul itself, as it goes about its self-forgetful business.

O.B., 77

Pleasure is of the body; joy is of the mind and heart.

P.R., 4

The power of rejoicing is always a fair test of a man's moral condition. No man can be happy on the outside who is already unhappy on the inside. . . . As sorrow is attendant on sin, so joy is the companion of holiness.

W.H., 24

To pass from sadness to joy requires a birth, a moment of travail and labor, for no one ever mounts to a higher level of life without death to the lower.

W.I., 51

Judaism

What would Christianity be without Jesus who came to the world from Israel?

What would the Church be without the twelve Jews who were Apostles of the Messiah?

What would Christianity be without the background of Abraham, Moses, Isaac, John the Baptist, and the prophets who announced the Messiah?

L.A., 125

Judas

The patron of those critics who finds things wrong with others because they themselves fail to do what is right, is Judas.

D.L., 117

. . . when Our Blessed Lord said the night of the Last Supper, "One of you is about to betray Me," eleven men leaned forward saying, "Is it I? Is it I? Is it I?" One man *pulled back* and said, "Is it I?" When one is falsely accused, he will advance toward the aggressor or the one who charges him wrongly; but when the charge is true, he will fall back, shrinking as it were from the truth of the accusation.

L.2, 204

Judges (Bleeding-Heart)

A Federal judge in Washington assailed what he considered to be "an unfortunate trend of judicial decisions which strain and stretch to give the guilty, not the same, but vastly *more* protection, than the law-abiding citizen." Bleeding hearts, some of whom are supposed to administer justice, are so concerned for criminals and terrorists that today the good citizens are considered off the reservation, as the new compassion exalts the guilty and condemns the innocent.

G.T., 28

Judgment

The truly happy person does not really care what others may think of him, for true glory consists in the judgment of God rather than in the judgment of men.

D.L., 15

Self-examination alone makes our judgments kindly.

D.L., 127

The morning after excessive drinking, the head with its hangover makes a judgment on intemperance, as during the night the sick stomach passes judgment on the food that was not good for digestion. As audiences make judgment on a play by their applause, so there is to be a final accountability for the thoughts and the words and deeds of every human heart. In vain is it to be expected that we who pass judgment constantly on others should not pass in judgment ourselves.

G.T., 46

It is a common human standard to judge virtues by the vices from which we abstain; and to find the wickedness of others an excuse for our own: "I am just as good as the next fellow."

L.A., 117

In England the judges wear wigs in court, to show that it is the law which is passing judgment, and not their own personal views. This is done in recognition of the truth all men suspect—that there is something impudent in allowing even the wisest among us to engage in pigeonholing our friends or cataloging our enemies.

O.B., 27

The judgment at death is something like being stopped by a motor-cop, except, thank heaven, the Good Lord is not as hard as the motor cops. When we are stopped, God does not say: "What kind of a car did you drive?" He is no respecter of persons. He asks: "How well did you drive? Did you obey the laws?"

P.R., 134

There are three different ways in which we may judge others: with our passions, our reason and our faith. Our passions induce us to love those who love us; our reason makes us love all people within certain limits; our faith makes us love everyone, including those who do us harm and who are our enemies.

W.I., 110

Judgment Day

For when the curtain goes down on the last day, and we respond to the curtain call of judgment, we will not be asked what part we played, but how well we played the part that was assigned to us.

M.T., 75

Justice

Previously when men's passions made them forget justice momentarily, they nevertheless wanted to return to justice when their passions subsided. They did wrong, but they never denied it was wrong. Today, on the contrary, nations not only violate the laws of justice, but they even deny there is justice.

D.D., 138

. . . a Justice which sees evil and does not punish it, is not Justice.

D.R., 65

Love without justice is sentimentality; justice without love is socialism.

M.P., 69

Juvenile Delinquency

The first step in the making of juvenile delinquency is philosophical and educational. It consists in teaching youth that there is no distinction between right and wrong; that the difference between good and bad is purely a "point of view" and that each one is the absolute standard of virtue and vice. Associated with this is the false psychological theory that the youth must never be told that there is such a thing as personal guilt; there are only social responses which are capable of being regulated and trained by technical sociologists. Thus a sense of responsibility, duty and justice to society are killed as blame is centered on environment, society, heredity or glands rather than the will of youth itself.

D.L., 101

K

Kafka, Franz

Kafka is not antimoral, nor anti-God. Kafka was just a modern soul who felt something of the punishment that the Godless soul was experiencing, and was able to describe it well, but could offer no solution. His characters are marionettes, either victims or executioners, because the world is dark and humble and devoid of moral rules.

L.2, 57

Kantianism and Comtism

The net result of the Kantian and Comtian outlook on the universe was the pragmatist theory that science is autonomous and self-contained, and the criterion is not truth but utility.

PH., II

Know Thyself

Few of us really know ourselves, and few ever want to know. We imagine ourselves to be very different from what we are. We wear a mask in public but seldom take it off when we are alone. Hence we think that our critics *always* misjudge us. We believe our friends are right when they praise us, and wrong when they criticize us. Most of our acquaintances could tell us faults about ourselves which we would deny most vociferously, and yet they might be only too true.

L.A., 79

If we are proud, covetous, conceited, selfish, lustful, constantly wanting our own way, it is far better to come face to face with our own ugliness than to live in a fool's paradise.

W.I., 22–23

Every man is stronger for knowing the worst he can about himself and then acting on that knowledge.

W.I., 23

Knowing

We have three ways of knowing: One is by our senses, such as the clasp of a hand. The second is by abstract ideas and scientific training, such as the science of physics. Over and above both feeling and intellect, there is another kind of knowledge which a husband and wife have after many years of married life—they have come to know one another by loving one another.

F.D., 42

Knowing versus Loving

When we know something, we bring it *down* to the level of our intelligence. Examples of abstract subjects must be given to children to suit the level of their minds. But when we love something, we always have to go *up* to meet it.

L.2, 173

Knowledge

Knowledge without love leads to conceit, intolerance and selfishness.

D.L., 37

True love with knowledge leads to deeper insights. Knowledge halts at the threshold of the temple; love enters in and worships.

D.L., 37

Knowledge is as necessary as light. In fact it is like light: it is in itself devoid of color, water, taste, and odor and it should be kept pure and without admixture. If it comes to us through the medium of prejudice, hate, or uncontrolled passions, it is discolored and adulterated.

L.5, 281

Knowing many things is different from knowing truth.

W.I., 19

Knowledge comes only with humility before the object which can bring us truth.

W.I., 120

L

Labor

No amount of piety in leisure hours can compensate for slipshod labor on the job. But any honest task, well done, can be turned into a prayer.

W.H., 54

Larynx

There are too many in America today who believe that the larynx is sacred, and that any attempt to throttle its vocalizations is an infringement on liberty.

F.G., 192

Lateness

One of the manifestations of the ego is the habit of being late for appointments.

T.T., 11

Laughter

The only time laughter is wicked is when it is turned against Him Who gave it.

L.C., 348

Laurels

No man is living who is resting on his own laurels, as no one is happy who says that he lives on his memories. Past laurels must be put aside as man must press forward to that supernal vocation to which he is called, forgetting the things that are behind.

W.H., 163

Law and Morality

Can we not see that if law is divorced from morality and religion, then treaties cease to be obligatory and begin to be mere arrangements, binding only so long as they are advantageous? Rob international justice of its roots in morality and treaties are hypothetical, not categorical; convenient tools, not honorable obligations, while law becomes an attorney's cloak woven from the flimsy fabric of legalistic phraseology artfully placed on the shoulders of arbitrary power.

D.V., 70

Law (Civil)

In our days when some politicians prostitute public office or else ally themselves with evil forces, they justify their wickedness on the ground that "they did nothing against the law." The only law for them becomes civil law, and their individual interpretation of it; never do they think of the moral law in their conscience, or the Ten Commandments.

W.I., 105

Lawbreaking

No one who over-drinks wills the headache, but he gets one; no man who sins wills frustration or loneliness of soul, but he feels it. In breaking a law we always suffer certain consequences which we never intended. God so made the world that certain effects follow certain causes.

D.V., 25

Laws (Natural)

What we call the natural laws, such as the laws of astronomy and the laws of physics and the laws of biology, are in reality so many reflections of the Eternal Reason of God. God made things to act in a certain way. In this sense the oak is a judgment on the acorn; the harvest is the judgment on the seed that was sown.

D.V., 23

Leader

One of the greatest tragedies that can happen to any civilization is for its leaders to become politicians.

D.L., 84

Leisure

The modern man has more leisure than the men of a century ago, but he knows less what to do with it.

W.I., 108–109

Lenin, Vladimir

Lenin . . . was a St. Francis in reverse, as St. Francis was a Lenin in reverse. Both started with the idea of violence: Lenin believed in social reform by violence to a class; St. Francis believed in social reform by violence to himself.

S.C., 92

Liberal

Every liberal is in revolt against the last revolt.

L.2, 45

They say they are looking for truth; yet if they ever met truth, they would drop dead.

L.2, 104

He changes his philosophy as he changes his clothes. On Monday, he lays down the tracks of materialism; on Tuesday, he reads a best seller, pulls up the old tracks, and lays the new tracks of an idealist; on Wednesday, his new roadway is Communistic; on Thursday, the new rails of Liberalism are laid; on Friday, he hears a broadcast and decides to travel on Freudian tracks; on Saturday, he takes a long drink to forget his railroading and, on Sunday, ponders why people are so foolish as to go to Church. Each day he has a new idol, each week a new mood.

P.S., 7

The intellectual world has suddenly rediscovered that man is a seat of conflict. Marx found conflict in society, Kierkegaard in the soul, Heidegger in man's being, and psychologists in the mind. To the credit of all of them, it must be said that they come much closer to an understanding of man than did the Liberals of the last few centuries, who taught that man was naturally good and progressive and on the high road to becoming a god without God.

P.S., 30

G. K. Chesterton, in his play *Magic,* tells of a duke who signed two checks. One check was to aid in the building of a large saloon; the second check was to aid the league opposing the building of the saloon. It was not long until he had the reputation of being "a very liberal-minded man."

T.T., 36

Liberal (Old and New)

The old liberal rebelled against taxation without responsibility; the new liberal wants the taxation as a handout without responsibility.

G.C., 56

Liberal versus Reactionary

A reactionary may be described as a man with two feet in a pair of shoes but he absolutely refuses to walk. A liberal has been very well described as one who has both feet firmly planted in mid-air.

L.2, 43

It is as easy to fall into the pit of being a reactionary as it is easy to fall into the hole of being a liberal—all one has to do is to go to an extreme.

L.4, 22

Liberalism

Liberalism defines freedom as the right to do whatever you please, and that is the way freedom is understood by 90% of young Americans educated in non-religious institutions. If freedom means that, it means anarchy.

G.W., 35

The danger today is in believing there are no sick people, there is only a sick society.

L.2, 186

Liberalism and Society

The traditional restraints and moral sanctions of society come to be regarded more and more as worthless, outworn taboos or as cruel checks placed upon individual egotism, which now goes under the name of freedom. A stage is eventually reached where there is no acknowledged limit to self-expression. The most traitorous deeds are defended as civil rights; the defense of even the natural law is ridiculed as "medieval." This lawlessness, if widespread, creates such confusion in society that a tyrant soon arises to organize the chaos through force. Thus is fulfilled the dictum of Dostoevski that "unlimited freedom leads to unlimited tyranny."

P.S., 165

Liberalism and Totalitarianism

Liberalism killed the end of living; Totalitarianism killed both the end and the means to it. Liberalism thwarted personality by restricting the development of man to individual acts of choice, by making each man a law unto himself. Totalitarianism frustrates personality by incarnating the end of man in the will of a dictator and identifying the perfection of each man with obedience to that arbitrary will. Liberalism forgot God; Totalitarianism forgets freedom and makes Caesar a God. Liberalism forgot freedom of perfection; Totalitarianism forgets both freedom of perfection and freedom of choice, and by ignoring choice ignores the right of each man to perfect himself as something beyond the race, the nation, and the class.

F.G., 244

Liberation

Liberation also means exemption from the horrendous experiences of poverty, injustice, and slavery, but above all, liberation means finding the truth in Christ. He was the only one who ever said, "I am the Truth." Truth and the person became identified and thereby truth became lovable. This is true liberation: "The truth will make you free."

L.L., 11

Liberation (Modern)

It is very likely that people will one day say that the flag has no mystery or meaning in our American life, nor is it a symbol of a piety or sacred loyalty. Then someone will write an article on the "Liberation of the American Flag" and plead that it should not only be flown above our heads but trampled beneath our feet; otherwise it is enslaved to one attitude.

O.B., 117

Liberation Theology

. . . the definition of Christianity is made so broad as to include not only those who are not Christians, but who may with reasonable certainty be Communists.

D.L., 181

Liberty

The bald fact the enemies of God must face is that modern civilization has conquered the world, but in doing so has lost its soul. And in losing its soul it will lose the very world it gained. Even our own so-called Liberal culture in these United States, which has tried to avoid complete secularization by leaving little zones of individual freedom, is in danger of forgetting that these zones were preserved only because religion was in their soul. And as religion fades so will freedom, for only where the spirit of God is, is there liberty.

C.P., 43

Liberty, correctly understood, is the right to choose between good things in order to develop the highest reaches of personality.

L.E., I

Liberty versus Justice

One of the greatest disasters that happened to modern civilization was for democracy to inscribe "liberty" on its banners instead of "justice." Because "liberty" was considered the ideal it was not long until some men interpreted it as meaning "freedom from justice."

D.D., 51

Lies

No one gets angrier at being told a lie than a habitual liar.

O.B., 28

Life

Life can be based on either of two assumptions. One is that the obstacles, trials and sorrows are not a part of the pattern of life. There must be all warp and no woof in fabric of existence. Hence, in the face of annoyances one must either seek flight from existence through alcohol or barbiturates, or else blame all that happens on others. From this flow discords, revolutions and wars. The second assumption is that everything that happens to us must be changed and transmuted by a Divine Vision so that, instead of defeating, it rather aids us to mount to higher levels of peace.

D.L., 81

There are other ways of begetting life, we must remember, than physically. The most chaste way that life is begotten, is the way in which thoughts and ideas are born in the mind.

L.A., 14

Life is monotonous if it has no goal or purpose. When we do not know why we are here or where we are going, then life is full of frustrations and unhappiness. When there is no goal or over-all purpose, people generally concentrate on motion. Instead of working toward an ideal, they keep changing the ideal and calling it "progress."

L.I, 2

With all our knowledge of chemistry we cannot make a human life in our laboratories because we lack the unifying, vivifying principle of a soul which comes only from God. Life is not a push from below; it is a gift from above. It is not the result of the necessary ascent of man, but the loving descent of God. It is not the term of Progress; it is the fruit of the Incarnation.

P., 9

To a great extent the world is what we make it. We get back what we give. If we sow hate, we reap hate; if we scatter love and gentleness we harvest love and happiness.

W.H., 134

Life (Modern)

Modern life is geared to the idea that beauty in a woman and strength in a man are permanent possessions. All the mechanics of modern advertising are directed to this lie.

T.M., 98

Liking and Loving

There is a world of difference between *loving* and *liking*. Liking is in the *emotion;* loving is in the *will*. Liking is not subject completely to our control, but love can be commanded. Liking is a kind of reaction like a hiccough; loving is a decision or a resolution. We cannot *like* everyone, but we can *love* everyone.

L.I, 166

Limits

Nature sets certain limits to *more* for your bodies. A boy's eyes are bigger than his stomach. There is a limit to bodily pleasures. They reach a point where they become a pain, as we become sickened of their own "too much." But there are no limits to the desires of your soul. They never reach a point of satiety. There are no limits to the truth you can know, to the life you can live, and to the love you can enjoy, and to the beauty you can experience.

P.R., 128

Loneliness

No one is lonely except he who is self-centered and who cuts himself off from communion with his fellow man.

E.I., 17

The basic cause of loneliness is the excessive desire to be loved, for this creates an atmosphere of lovelessness. The more we seek to be loved, the less we are loved. The less we are loved, the less lovable we become. And the less lovable we become, the less capable we become of loving anyone else. Like a bird caught in a net, we deepen our tragedy.

F.D., 25

Love

The more intense the love, the less we think of a sacrifice involved to secure what we love.

D.L., 35

The measure of our love for anything is the amount of pain we are willing to suffer to gain the object loved, or to avoid what is offensive and wrong.

D.L., 106

Love has two terms: He Who loves and He Who is loved. In love the two are reciprocal. I love and I am loved. Between me and the one I love there is a bond. It is not my love; it is not his love; it is our love; the mysterious resultant of two affections, a bond which enchains, and an embrace wherein two hearts leap with but a single joy.

D.R., 31

Love is not just an affirmation, but a negation; it implies sacrifice— a surrender of our will, of our selfish interests, for the good of the other. It looks not to the lover's pleasure, but to the happiness of the beloved.

G.W., 16

Love may be defined as mutual self-giving and self-outpouring which ends in self-recovery.

H.C., 64

Love, I say, forgives everything except one thing, and that is the refusal to love.

H.C., 98

Love is the key to the mystery. Love by its very nature is not selfish, but generous. It seeks not its own, but the good of others. The measure of love is not the pleasure it gives—that is the way the world judges it—but the joy and peace it can purchase for others.

R.S., 36

Those who do not yet love one another deeply have need of words; those who deeply love, thrive on silences.

T.M., 32

No love ever mounts to a higher level without a touch of the Cross.

T.M., 52

To want to be more than we are is earthly; to want to be less than we are by spending ourselves on others is heavenly.

T.T., 54

The . . . mystery is not why we love, but why we are loved. It is easy to understand why we love because of our incompleteness and our radical dissatisfaction apart from goodness. But why anyone should love us is the mystery, for we know when we look at our real selves how very little there is to love.

W.H., 76

The great mystery of life is really not that we want to be loved, but that we are loved. We need love because we are imperfect; but why anyone should love the imperfect is not easy to understand. That is why all lovers consider themselves unworthy. The beloved is on a pedestal, the lover is on his knees professing his unworthiness. Love always comes as an undeserved gift.

W.H., 104

Love (Divine)

God does not love us because we are lovely or lovable; His love exists not on account of our character, but on account of His. Our highest experience is *responsive,* not initiative. And it is only because we are loved by Him that we are lovable.

C.I., 9

Love (Suffering)

Suffering love alone can bring us to our senses and the real meaning of life.

L.4, 240

Love (Woman's)

Woman loves differently from man. Man is driven by the love of pleasure; woman by the pleasure of love; man has to have his body satisfied; woman has to have her soul satisfied; she loves because of what love does for the enrichment and meaning of her soul. She does not want the great flood tides of feeling breaking over the dam of personality, but the thousand little trickles of the fountain of affection. That is why her love is far more constant than that of man. She is capable of more fidelity than man because by nature her love is less intermittent and also because she is not ready for love until it can mean total and complete dedication.

L.5, 122

Love (Young)

Many young people who think they fall in love are actually falling in love with the *experience* of love. Because the other person gives a "glow," qualities are attributed to him or her which do not exist. She marries a "hero" and lives with a husband; he marries a "goddess" and lives with a wife.

G.T., 23

Loyalties

No Liberal was ever willing to incommode himself for Liberalism, but Communists are very willing to sacrifice themselves for Communism. In this day of intense loyalties the sleek repose of Christians who will not sacrifice themselves for the things of God cannot meet the new challenge. It will take a great faith in Christ to put down faith in anti-Christ; it will take nothing less than the sacrifice of the Cross to conquer the sacrifice of those who crucify.

C.C., 198

Lust

Lust is not sex—for sex is purely biological and is a God-given capacity; nor is it love, which finds one of its lawful expressions in sex. Lust is the isolation of sex from true love. There is no passion which more quickly produces slavery than lust—as there is none whose perversions more quickly destroy the power of the intellect and the will.

L.H., 68

Luxury

Today millions of men and women consider that their happiness is destroyed if they must get along without a few things of which their grandfathers had never dreamed. Luxuries have become necessities to them; and the more things a man needs in order to be happy, the more he has increased his chances of disappointment and despair.

O.B., 78

M

MacArthur, Douglas

He always looked you straight in the eye when he talked and gave the impression of authority and power. I personally believe that he was one of the greatest characters that America has ever produced. Among the reflections he offered at dinner were these: he wished he had eight hundred Catholic missionaries for every one now working in Japan to bring that country to Christianity. The world struggle, he said, is not economic or political but religious and theological; it is either God or atheism.

A., 141

Macbeth

. . . the way of Macbeth and the way of Lady Macbeth, one finds not the best, not the mediocre, but the samples of the worst features of Western civilization and Communism. The basest exponents of the philosophy of Western civilization are those who believe in relativism and consent to evil on the ground that there is no judgment and no moral law.

T.T., 86

Magdalen's Gift

To value only what can be *"sold"* is to defile what is truly precious. The innocent joy of childhood, the devotedness of a wife, the self-sacrificing service of a daughter—none of these have an earthly market. To reduce everything to the dirty scales of economic values is to forget that some gifts, like Mary's, are so precious that the heart that offers them will be praised as long as time endures.

D.L., 118

The Majority

When struggle, battle and sacrifice are demanded, the majority complain and clamor for going back to Egypt or spiritual slavery.

M.P., 141

Man

Man is the only being in the world who can reflect, and hence the only one who can turn back upon himself, be angry with himself, be pleased with himself, contemplate his own thoughts, perceive the difference between what he is and what he seems, his own worth and what others attribute to him. He is the only creature in the universe who can look upon himself as in a mirror and see himself as others see him, and even sit, as it were, on another planet and let his feet hang over, contemplating off in the distance a planet which happens to be his very self.

C., 57

Man is the only creature that has a hand that is creative, and with it he puts the stamp of his mind upon stone and gold, founds his sovereignty of civilization, and comforts his fellowman.

F.D., 111

Man is a mystery even to himself.

P.N., 222

. . . man is not an evolution but a revolution. He may be an animal but he also has a soul. He is the only animal in the world that is not a domestic animal. Every other animal in this world seems to belong to this world and is content with it. Man is the only wild animal in the sense that he is not domestic in his longings and aspirations; because of his soul, he has an infinite reach toward the infinite life, love, and truth of the God Who made him.

O.E., 318

In the Days of Darwin, blind thinkers went to man and since he felt like an animal they said he must be an animal, and therefore should be treated as an animal. Thus we had jurists like Justice Holmes of the Supreme Court defining man as a "cosmic ganglion." If man is only a ganglion why should we go to war to prevent Hitler from making mincemeat of ganglia?

P.W., 83

If we are only animals and not moral creatures of God, then certainly act like animals; then certainly permit divorces, and a pharmacopoeia of devices, prophylactic and eugenic, to cultivate the animal that man is; make it a universe where the ethics of man are no different from the ethics of the barnyard and the stud.

P.W., 123

The fact is, man is not naturally and indefinitely perfectible; left to himself man is capable of being a fool. This in simple language comes close to what we mean by the doctrine of original sin. If man is the highest thing that evolution has thrown on the shores of our centuries, then he has no value in his own right. A philosophy that makes him can break him.

W.W., 67

Man and Christ

Now we hasten to add that just as the life of a human organism does not destroy the individual cell-life of its million of cells, so neither does the mystical body of Christ destroy the individuality of the members. We all share the individual life of Christ, and yet there is no absorption, no merging of offices; there still remains diversity of ministries but the same spirit. There is unity but there is also multiplicity.

O.E., 246

Man and Cosmos

We know too much about matter to be materialists; we know too much about stars to think we are but star-dust. The galaxy of suns and starry worlds may boast of bulk and size and speed, but we too have our boast: Christ walked *our* earth.

O.E., 29

Man and Machine

. . . the difference between a machine and a man is the difference between *must* and *ought*.

H.C., II

Man and the World

Nothing ever happens to the world which does not first happen inside man.

W.H., 167

Man (Bad versus Evil)

A bad man will do wrong things, such things as cheat, steal, slander, murder, and violate, but he will still admit the law. He will get off the road, but he will not throw away the road map. An evil man, on the contrary, may not do any of these bad things; he is concerned not with the concrete but with the abstract. His desire is to completely destroy goodness, religion, morality in a mad bigotry. He would justify in his life the false desire of Nietzsche: "Evil be thou my good." He seeks for a transvaluation of values in which night is day and day is night, good is evil and evil good.

L.4, 48

Man (Common)

The common man may not be socially proper, he may not have a college education, he may not know how to act in our drawing rooms, but he holds the future in his hands. Both the Church and civilization will draw their strength from such a man.

P., 68

Man (Communist)

Man in Communism has ceased to exist; he is socialized, communized, and dissolved even to the very core of his being. He has no will but the will of the State; no thought but the thought of the Collectivity; no blood but the blood of the race; no rights but the rights of the nation. Mystically submerged body and soul, he no longer has life in God but only life in the collectivity. He has been transubstantiated not into a divinized creature of God, but into a mechanized tool capable of producing the maximum of capital in the minimum of time. Man has ceased to exist; there remains only numbers, instruments, quantity, tools, and all are functions of the mass. There is now no God but Caesar.

C.C., 62

Man (Decline of)

The liquidation of man in the modern world will not be arrested simply by protests of horror. We must recognize . . . and begin affirming, in the United States, the worth of a person as a creature of God.

L.1, 69

Man (Forgotten)

Our problem today then is the problem of the Forgotten Man— not the forgotten man in the sense of the man who is unemployed, or hungry; but forgotten man in the sense of forgotten human dignity, forgotten human worth, forgotten divine destiny, forgotten personality, forgotten power to rise above the state and the collective to commune with the Life and Truth and Love which is God. This is the real Forgotten man of our day—the man who can enter into himself and find down in the depths of his soul that he was made for God and only God can make him remembered.

P., 35

Man (Free)

No free man can be made good against his will.

C.C., 2

Man (Humble)

Humility is truth. A humble man neither praises nor belittles himself. Underestimation can be as false as overestimation.

O.B., 66

The humble man makes room for progress; the proud man believes he is already there.

O.B., 66

He is never discouraged, for discouragement is a form of pride.

O.B., 67

When the humble man is treated badly he does not complain for he knows that he is treated better than he deserves.

W.H., 18

The rich man who is humble helps the poor rather than the revolutionists who use the poor to bomb their ways to Stalinist thrones.

W.I., 12

The humble man is not a rigid exacter of things to which he has no undoubted right; he is always ready to overlook the faults of others knowing that he has so many.

W.I., 12

Man (Learned)

A learned man need never carry the books which he has authored so that everyone can see them; but an ignorant man who wishes to appear learned must use words so long that they actually ought to appear in serial form.

T.T., 12

Man (Mass)

The new man is the mass-man, who no longer prizes his individual personality, but who seeks to be submerged in the collectivity or crowd.

He is without originality of judgment; does no other reading except what is found in a daily newspaper, or picture magazine, or an occasional novel. He has only a different point of view to give on a common subject, but no new principle or solution.

W.H., 164

The perfect symbol of the impersonal mass-man is the social security number, which completes his alienation from himself.

W.H., 165

Man (Modern)

. . . modern man is drifting toward the assumption that he cannot do anything wrong.

D.L., 168

Man is now a tool for dictators, a pawn for tyrants, a "sucker" for propaganda, a contradiction to be consumed. In reality there is no longer man because there is nothing that gives man dignity.

D.L., 178

The case for modern man can be better understood when it is realized that in this century, he has hit the bottom of his soul. The cheap Liberalism, the spineless indifference, the false tolerance which failed to distinguish between good and evil, night and day, wrong and right, did but make man inactive and unhappy.

D.L., 181

The modern man has already one-half the condition of salvation: he is miserable.

L.2, 57

Our modern man has three forces or fears: fear of death, fear of the meaninglessness of life, and the fear of being found out.

O.B., 46

Modern man would be far happier if he would take a little time off to meditate.

O.B., 60

We see this in the intellectual history of the proud man of the twentieth century; his abandonment of the philosophy of evolution and inevitable progress was succeeded by the philosophy of despair, defeat, and fear. Two generations ago, he was about to be a god; today, that god is being psychoanalyzed to find out why he feels "like the devil."

P.S., 222

. . . it has been said Christianity does not suit the modern man, therefore scrap Christianity. Now let us say, Christianity does not suit modern man, therefore let us scrap modern man.

P.W., 98–99

Religion, they judge by their own standards, and whenever they write on the subject, their articles are entitled: "My idea of religion." Never do they seek to know God's idea of religion. Their own preconceived prejudices constitute the norm of judgment.

S.C., 61

As the Soviet world is a closed society allowing no influences from the outside world to pass into it except science, which it can turn against the Western world, so the modern minds allow nothing from the spiritual universe to penetrate into its closed circle.

T.T., 16

Never before have men possessed so many time-saving devices. Never before have they had so little time for leisure or repose.

W.H., 55

He seeks to be influenced rather than to influence, is sensitive to propaganda, to the excitations of publicity and generally has one favorite columnist who does his thinking for him.

W.H., 164

His beliefs of right and wrong change like the weathercock.

W.H., 165

To break his solitude he has recourse to an ersatz communion with others, through night clubs, parties and collective distractions. But from each of these he returns more lonely than before, finally believing with Sartre that "hell is others."

W. H., 165

Man (Nature of)

The nature of man is a spiritual and not an economic question. Our political and economic difficulties are merely symptoms of something more seriously wrong; namely, the nature of man and his relation both to his neighbor and to his God.

C.C., 64

Man (Non-attached)

The finished man or the perfected man is the non-attached man, non-attached to a craving for power, publicity and possessions; non-attached to anger, ambition and avarice; non-attached to selfish desires, lusts and bodily sensations. The practice of non-attachment to the things which stunt our soul is one of the things meant by "the Hour."

S.W., 82

Man on the Street

If I wanted a good moral judgment about the war, I should a thousand times prefer to get it from a garage man, a filling station attendant, a WPA worker, a grocer's clerk, or a delivery boy, than from twenty-three Ph.D. Professors I know about in just one American University.

G.C., 38

Man (Problem of)

The great concern facing civilization today is not the problem of unemployment, not finances, not production or consumption, not free trade or world relations or even property rights. The problem of the hour is the *problem of man*. Human dignity is at stake; the value of a human personality is being questioned.

C.C., 58

Man (Proud)

The man who is not hard on himself for his faults will always be hard on others. The proud man, who never admits he is wrong, loves to blame servants, golf clubs, the driver in "that car" and the Electra complex of his grandmother.

D.L., 106

Man (Public)

Notice how often today men in public life accuse one another of "lying." Why is it they never speak of truth? May it not be that they studied in the same school as Pilate and asked "What is Truth?" and then turn their backs on it.

W.I., 123

Man (Self-seeking)

The man who is self-seeking eventually ends up by hating himself. That is why such a person often tries to "get away from himself," through alcohol, dissipation, and drugs. The self one has to live

with can be one's own greatest punishment. To be left forever with
that self which we hate is hell.

Man (Spirit of)

Human beings do not die for things alone but for what they believe about things. No scientist ever died for a bug. He died for the
sake of humanity, which that bug was stinging. No one ever laid
down his life for the stars, but some will lay down their lives for the
truth that the stars bring. It is, therefore, not matter but the spirit
that summons the best in man, the spirit of learning, the spirit of
truth, the spirit of love—and all these are above the individual man
in dignity and worth.

O.E., 262

Man (Theories of)

There are ultimately only two possible theories to account for the
nature and the origin of man: One is that the life of man is a push
from below; the other, that the life of man is a gift from above.
The one is that man is wholly of the earth earthly; the other that
he is partly of the heaven heavenly. The second is the Christian
conception: man is not a risen beast, he is rather a kind of fallen
angel. His origin is hidden not in the slime and dust of prehistoric
forests, but in the clear daylight of Paradise where he communed
with God; his origin goes back not to cosmic forces, but to divine
grace. According to this conception, man is supposed to act not
like a beast because he came from one, but like God because he is
made to His own image and likeness.

L.A., 64–65

Man (Vain)

Vain people like to prove themselves right, especially in argument. What is important is not the *truth* of things, but their being *right*.

L.2, 71-72

Man versus Machine

. . . no machine is capable of nonsense.

L.4, 126

Man (Whole)

The distance between spirituality and social action is not as great as many believe. Scripture does not reveal a spiritual man or a secular man. It speaks only of a whole man—integrated by the salvation that Christ brings.

M.P., 243

Man has no organic functions isolated from his soul.

T.M., 4

Man (Wise)

The wise man knows *one thing,* which is Goodness, and all else is unified in it.

W.H., 29

Manners

Politeness is a way of showing externally the internal regard we have for others. Good manners are the shadows cast by virtues.

O.B., 177

Marriage

Wives cannot understand why others enjoy their husbands' company, and neither can husbands understand why others find their wives so charming. This is because each can tell the same old stories to a new audience. Marriage is like television: it eats up the material, and no one wants to hear it again.

L.4, 184

One's partner must never be an instrument of one's will; rather, in marriage, the partner is a limit to one's will. The other person is not to be regarded as being like a subjugated colony, in which one may suppress governments and customs by one's own will. This is egotism, and egotism in marriage is assassination. Purification is not to be had just by silence, for silence is egotism. The taking of love's stronghold comes after the siege of self, in which individuality and selfishness are crushed.

L.5, 291

Man cannot be happy if he is satiated; our zest comes from the fact that there are doors not yet opened, veils not yet lifted, notes that have not been struck. If a "love" is only physical, marriage will bring the romance to an end: the chase is ended, and the mystery is solved. Whenever any person is thus taken for granted, there is a loss of the sensitivity and delicacy which are the essential condition of friendship, joy, and love in human relations. Marriage is no exception; one of its most tragic outcomes is mere possession without desire.

O.B., 97

Too many married people expect their partner to give . . . an eternal ecstasy.

T.M., 35

The death of illusions is not the death of love. The great advantage of the vow is that it holds people together during this temporary stress and trial, in order to attain a more lasting love.

T.T., 108

Marriage Counselor

If one has marital difficulties and is inclined to leave the spouse, the worst person to go to is a psychiatrist who is already divorced and re-married.

W.I., 37

Martyrdom (Age of)

More people have suffered because of their religion since 1917 than in the first three centuries of the Christian era. Whether we know it or not, we live in the Age of the Great Martyrdom.

D.L., 162

Marxism

Marx and Communism have turned the supremacy of the species into the supremacy of the class. Once admitted, it follows that what happens to an individual person is of no concern. The revolutionary class of Communism alone has value. Communism is an aggressive religion of the species.

L.I, 68

Mary

It was really the last lesson in detachment which Jesus had been teaching her these many years, and the first lesson of the new attachment. Our Lord had been gradually "alienating," as it were, His affections from His Mother, not in the sense that she was to love Him less, or that He was to love her less, but only in the sense that she was to love *us more*. She was to be detached from motherhood in the flesh, only to be more attached to that greater motherhood in the spirit.

C.M., 45

Mary is the refuge of sinners. She who is Virgin Most Pure is also the Refuge of Sinners. She knows what sin is, not by the experience of its falls, not by tasting its bitter regrets, but by seeing what it did to her Divine Son.

V.V., 39

. . . she is what God wanted us all to be, she speaks of herself as the Eternal blueprint in the Mind of God, the one whom God loved before she was a creature. She is even pictured as being with Him not only at creation, but before creation. She existed in the Divine Mind as an Eternal Thought before there were any mothers. She is the Mother of mothers—SHE IS THE WORLD'S FIRST LOVE.

W.L., II

Let those who think that the Church pays too much attention to Mary give heed to the fact that Our Blessed Lord Himself gave ten times as much of His life to her as He gave to His Apostles.

W.L., 88

The Mass

The Mass is the temporalization in time and localization in space of Calvary.

M.P., 148

The Mass causes the historically past events of His life to emerge here and now in their eternal reality. Here there is no subjective recollection, but the re-emerging of Christ's Death and Resurrection into our contemporaneous situation. The Lord opens the bridge between the eternal and the temporal; that which was past is resummoned for active operation here and now.

M.P., 148

Mass Media

No one knows who is responsible for group opinion; the authoritarianism is anonymous—it is always "they."

O.B., 137

Masses

The world is still mobilizing, still ignoring the human, still counting bodies instead of souls, still thinking of Poverty instead of the Poor, and of the *masses* instead of man.

C.C., 36

The mob is almost always in favor of the crucifixion of Christ. The difference between democracy and mass movements is this: in a democracy, the individuals are self-determined; in a mass-movement the determination comes from outside the individuals through leaders with bull horns or the Pharisees who moved among the crowd before the Fortress of Antonio to shout for the Death of Christ. Even though "everybody" was for the elimination of Christ, the majority was not right.

M.P., 140

Materialism

The real case against the new materialism must be a theological one. Doctrine must be invoked to combat doctrine. This is certain. Unless we can give men of the western world a faith to combat the false faith, the fanatical disciples of world revolution will capture and inflame the loyalty of millions, and we shall be destroyed by what is false within.

C.P., 98

The more materialistic a civilization is, the more it is in a hurry.

W.I., 134

Materialist

Those who deny the immortality of the soul, almost always substitute for it the immortality of the means of subsistence.

W.H., 28

. . . the more things a man needs in order to be happy, the more he has increased his chances of disappointment and despair.

W.H., 43

Maternity

There is a close connection between saving our souls and begetting life. . . . The pains which a woman bears in labor help to expiate the sins of mankind, and draw their meaning from the Agony of Christ on the Cross. Mothers are, therefore, not only co-creators with God; they are co-redeemers with Christ in the flesh.

T.M., 158

Matrimony

Matrimony crushes selfishness, first of all, because it merges individuals into a corporate life in which neither lives for self but for the other; it crushes selfishness also because the very permanence of marriage is destructive of those fleeting infatuations, which are born with the moment and die with it; it destroys selfishness, furthermore, because the mutual love of husband and wife takes them out of themselves into the incarnation of their mutual love, their other selves, their children; and finally it narrows selfishness because the rearing of children demands sacrifice, without which, like unwatered flowers, they wilt and die.

C.B., 41–42

Matter and Man

One moment a modern prophet tells us that man is great because he has evolved from matter: then in the next moment he tells us that he is nothing because matter is bigger than he is. . . . They cannot have evolution of man from matter and the domination of matter over man, at one and the same time. Either evolution of man from matter, or the supremacy of matter over man, must be given up. The two theories are contradictory. It is nonsense to sing Swinburne's hymn, "Glory to man in the highest, for man is the master of all," and then the next moment let the "all" master the man and immerse him in the very matter from whence he has risen. Such theorists cannot eat their cake and have it.

O.E., 24

The Mediocre

The mediocre are always self-satisfied and boast that they have done enough. That is because they judge themselves by their neighbors.

L.4, 209

Mediocrity

The world is suffering from the nemesis of mediocrity.

D.L., 96

Humility is required to challenge mediocrity; one must be ready to brave the taunts of those who knock anyone in the head who raises himself above the level of the masses. Mediocrity can be a terrific form of tyranny, and it has a thousand and one penalties for those who forsake the external standards for an inward change of heart to a line of conduct above the level.

W.I., 23

Meditation

Meditation allows one to suspend the conscious fight against external diversions by an internal realization of the presence of God. It shuts out the world to let in the Spirit. It surrenders our own will to the impetus of the Divine Will. It turns the searchlight of Divine Truth on the way we think, act, and speak, penetrating beneath the layers of our self-deceit and egotism. It summons us before the Bar of Divine Justice, so that we may see ourselves as we really are, and not as we like to think we are.

L.H., 151

Meekness

Which is right—the violence of Communism or the meekness of Christ? Communism says meekness is weakness. But that is because it does not understand the meaning of Christian meekness. Meekness is not cowardice; meekness is not an easy-going temperament, sluggish and hard to arouse; meekness is not a spineless passivity which allows everyone to walk over us. No! Meekness is self-possession. That is why the reward of meekness is possession.

C.B., 6

Memory

Today there seems to be a conspiracy against the noble faculty of memory.

W.I., 124

Memory is the autobiography of our lives, and though we cover the pages with barbiturates, the indelible record remains.

W.I., 125

Hidden in this retentive power of memory may also be the basis of what will be our final judgment, for what is memory but an infallible autobiography? As at the end of the day the business man takes out of the cash register a record of all the debits and the credits, so at the end of life the memory offers the basis of how we shall be judged.

W.I., 163–164

The memory has the peculiar trick of never asking our permission for anything it shoots up into consciousness; sometimes the more displeasing the ideas are, and the harder we try to forget them, the quicker and the more often they flash before our eyes. It is a psychological fact that the more the mind fears a thing, the more that fearful thing comes like a ghost out of the past to torture it.

W.I., 164

Men

Men cannot stand weakness. Men are, in a certain sense, the weaker sex. There is nothing that so much unnerves a man as a woman's tears. Therefore men need the strength and the inspiration of women who do not break in a crisis. They need someone not prostrate at the foot of the Cross, but standing, as Mary stood.

S.W., 13

"Merciful"

There are some crimes the tolerance of which is equivalent to consent to their wrong. Those who ask for the release of murderers, traitors, and the like, on the grounds that we must be "merciful, as Jesus was merciful," forget that that same Merciful Saviour also said that He came not to bring peace, but the sword.

W.H., 182

Mercy

. . . *mercy is the perfection of justice.* Mercy does not come first, and then justice; but rather justice first, then mercy.

W.H., 182

As we show mercy, we shall receive mercy. We harvest what we sow.

W.I., 111

Mercy (Divine)

The Divine Mercy did not identify the traitor, for Our Lord hid from the others the identity of the betrayer. The practice of the world which loves to spread scandals, even those which are untrue, is here reversed in the hiding of what is true. When they saw Judas leave, the others assumed that he went on a mission of charity.

P.N., 223

Mercy Killing

Is "unmerciful killing" wrong? (Some call it "mercy killing," but since killing is murder, it is unmerciful.) Unmerciful killing is wrong because a person has a soul that came from God. Not only may we not kill the aged or our political opponents; we may not even kill those who recommend unmerciful killing. For us, their rights come from God.

L.I, 213

Middle Age

In middle age a man begins to know himself, and to find out one's limitations is always an occasion for sorrow. Youth looks forward in hope, expectation, and promise; middle age sees that not all dreams and hopes come true.

O.B., 192

Milton, John

Milton was a liberal who favored a free press and protested against licensing of books; and then when a handsome salary was offered him he reacted against his liberalism and became an official censor of books.

G.C., 56

Mind (Modern)

There can be no health of soul or body while there is a moral conflict within. The modern mind thought it got rid of hell but found it within. A psychoanalyst can sublimate; God alone can give peace.

L.A., 81

In other generations the mind had problems; the mind of today *is* a problem.

P.S., 212

Mirth

Mirth is short and transient, while cheerfulness is fixed and permanent. Mirth is like a flash of lightning; cheerfulness, like daylight. A merry person laughs, a cheerful person smiles. Mirth always requires the companionship of others to feed upon—social excitement, noise, jests, wisecracks, stories; but cheerfulness exists even when one is alone.

G.T., 147

Missing Link

If the modern mind were asked what thing in the world it would like most to discover, it would probably answer: the missing link. Every now and then we hear of its discovery—but it is only a rumor. The most annoying feature of the missing link is that it is missing.

E.G., 129

Modernism

Modernism is no more logical than a sect called "Three O'Clockism," which would adapt our gods and our morals to our moods at three o'clock.

O.E., 79

Modernity

The future conflict of the world will not be between Religion and Science, or between "rugged individualism" and Socialism, but between a society which is spiritual and a society which is mechanical; between a society which adores God, and a society which claims to be God; between a society which absorbs man for secular ends, and a society which respects personality and uses the secular as a means to eternal ends. The world must make the choice. . . . Men will enlist on one side or the other; we must battle either for brotherhood in Christ, or comradeship in anti-Christ.

C.C., 55

In religious matters, the modern world believes in indifference. Very simply, this means it has no great loves and no great hates; no causes worth living for and no causes worth dying for. It counts its virtues by the vices from which it abstains, asks that religion be easy and pleasant, sneers the term "mystic" at those who are spiritually inclined, dislikes enthusiasm and loves benevolence, makes elegance the test of virtue and hygiene the test of morality, believes that one may be too religious but never too refined. It holds that no one ever loses his soul, except for some great and foul crime such as murder. Briefly, the indifference of the world includes no true fear of God, no fervent zeal for His honor, no deep hatred of sin, and no great concern for eternal salvation.

H.C., 26–27

The Era of Substitution has behind it three great revolutions: the religious revolution which uprooted man from responsibility to a spiritual community; the French Revolution which isolated man from responsibility to a political community or the State; and the Industrial Revolution and Liberalism which isolated man from all responsibility to the social community or the common good. Such is the essence of our secularist culture: the supremacy of the individual man.

P.W., 17

Never before in the history of the world was there so much knowledge; and never before so little coming to the knowledge of the Truth. Never before so much straining for life; never before so many unhappy lives. Never before so much science; never before was it used so for the destruction of human life.

S.P., 81–82

Monastery

The grating in a Carmelite monastery is not to keep the sisters in, but to keep the world out.

W.L., 142

Moral Landscapes

Moral landscapes are something like physical landscapes; that is why we believe that in retrospect the rough has become the soft, and the harsh the sweet. It could very well be that the disgust with which men feel the shocks and buffeting of the generation in which they live makes them falsely conclude that past days were better.

One notices this in the recently dead. How quickly the defects and the failings and even the vices of the dead seem to fade away with the passing of life. When friends and relatives were close to them, they saw faults. When they look at them now as those who have passed, all of the hidden goodness begins to appear.

G.T., 45

Moral Order

. . . if there is no Moral Order dependent on God, then any man is a fool for being true to his contract.

P.W., 123

Moral Relativism

The disrespect for authority which is the outgrowth of the stupidity that every individual is his own determinant of right and wrong has now become an epidemic of lawlessness.

W.H., 95

Modern man has become passive in the face of evil. He has so long preached a doctrine of false tolerance; has so long believed that right and wrong were only differences in a point of view, that now when evil works itself out in practice he is paralyzed to do anything against it.

W.H., 168

Morality

Our social structure, then, must one day admit the fallacy of "business is business"; it must judge its economic policies not by their feasibility but by their morality; and it must confess that economics and politics are but branches of moral theology and philosophy, i.e., they can be sinful if they violate the ultimate end of man. The moral necessity of man's attaining the full perfection of his personality circumscribes human action in the domestic, political, economic, and religious spheres.

C.C., 158

. . . the only condition upon which morality is possible is freedom.

D.R., 43–44

Anyone is free to deny morality, but he is not free to escape the effects of its violation. Sin is written on faces, in the brain, it is seen in the shifting eyes and the hidden fears of night.

W.H., 117

Morality (Western Bourgeois)

In the domain of morality, is it not an accepted principle of our Western bourgeois world that there is no absolute distinction between right and wrong rooted in the eternal order of God, but that they are relative and dependent entirely upon one's point of view? Hence when the Western world wishes to decide what is right and wrong even in certain moral matters, it takes a poll—forgetful that the majority never makes a thing right. . . . The first poll of public opinion taken in history of Christianity was on Pilate's front porch, and it was wrong.

C.C., 50

Mortician

Today's morticians make death look like life; they pretend that all that it involves is a little sleep, after which everyone will wake up on an eternal shore which has no passport regulations.

P.S., 197

Mortification

We should never let a day pass without doing three small mortifications, for example, not taking that extra cigarette or that second lump of sugar. Thus do we possess ourselves instead of being possessed by things. When these mortifications are done in the name of Our Lord, they become a source of great merit as well.

L.A., 98

. . . let it not be thought that mortification is a sign of weakness; rather it is a sign of power: it is the will controlling itself, submitting itself to defeat at its own hands, in order to win its finest victory; it is the making of the dead self a stepping stone to better things and the conquest of self the condition of the victory which brings everlasting peace and joy with God.

H.C., 38

Mother

Why is it that children, when they have a grief, will run to the mother rather than to the father? It is because the mother knows trouble better than the father; she has companioned more with pain, has more often passed through its cycles, and in giving birth has gone down to the very edge of death.

O.B., 45

No mother was ever favorably known to the world except through her children.

T.M., 231

Motherhood

Not only a woman's days, but her nights—not only her mind, but her body must share in the Calvary of motherhood. That is why women have a surer understanding of the doctrine of redemption than men have: they have come to associate the risk of death with life in childbirth, and to understand the sacrifice of self to another through the many months preceding it.

W.H., 87

Mother-in-law

. . . it should be remarked in defense of all mothers-in-law that St. Peter remained the truest friend of Our Blessed Lord, despite the fact that Our Lord cured his mother-in-law.

L.4, 41

Mystery (Divine)

The mystery of the Incarnation is that the Godhead dwelt in the Body; the mystery of Atonement is hidden in One offering of the Body of Christ; the mystery of sanctification is that the Holy Spirit dwells in and sanctifies the Body too.

P.N., 256

Mysticism

. . . if God is given by mere feeling, why is it that not every one believes in the existence of God?

G.I., 38

Myth (Modern)

A consequence of modern irrationality is the glorification of the myth, which Hitler has rather correctly defined as a slogan for evoking mass-enthusiasm. There is the myth of "race" in Germany, the myth of "class" in Russia, the myth of "nation" in Italy. In totalitarian states, the myth finds its most common expression in marching. Vast armies of men, boys, and girls are seen tramping— going nowhere, never being told where they are going, and soon beginning to care less. It is mass action without reason.

D.D., 5

N

Nakedness

Excessive adornments and an inordinate love of comforts are a proof of our inner nakedness.

P.N., 5

Nature

All nature testifies to the necessity of judgment. Everywhere below man nature reveals itself as passing sentence on those who refuse to obey her laws. We need only look around us in the hospitals, prisons, and asylums to see that nature, like a judge seated in judgment, is squaring her accounts with those who violate her laws. If the body has abused itself by excess, nature takes revenge and passes the judgment of disease and infirmity.

H.C., 79

Nature and Man

The forces of nature know no morality; it is men who use or abuse their powers.

W.H., 158

Nazism

Nazism is not negative like Communism. Communism is anti-religious; Nazism is not; it is very religious except that its religion is diabolical. There is only one word to describe how it grafted violence onto legality and that is in the phrase of Rauschning: "The Revolution of Nihilism."

P.W., 29

Need

There is a world of difference between what we need and what we want. We need those things which are essential for a normal, comfortable human existence; but we want more than that. Our needs are quickly satisfied, but our wants rarely.

S.V., 64

Neglect (Spiritual)

As the arm of a man, which is never called into exercise, loses its strength by degrees, and its muscles and its sinews disappear, even so the powers which God gave us, when unexercised, fail and fade from us.

M.U., 42

Neighbor

It is not of great moment to be constantly asking ourselves if we love our neighbor. What is important is to act out that love.

D.L., 29

The biblical command is not "Like thy neighbor," but "Love thy neighbor." Not every neighbor is likable, but every neighbor is lovable. It is hard to like certain neighbors who step on toes and make funny noises when they eat soup, but one can love them.

F.D., 89

The more Christian a soul is, the more it sees itself responsible for its neighbor's sins.

P.S., 223

A neighbor may be poor; he may speak ungrammatical English; he may smell of garlic, and he may not like us, but on the inside, his soul may be far more pleasing to God than our own.

T.T., 16

Other people are like a mirror which reflects back on us the kind of image we cast.

W.H., 134

. . . judge the neighbor by his best moments rather than by his worst.

W.I., 111

Most people demand of their neighbor much more than God demands of them.

W.I., 112

Neophilia

. . . the modern world embraces every new fad and fancy in the intellectual order, simply because it is new.

M.T., 62

Neurosis

It is the boredom of living in tombs without a regeneration which is the general neurosis of our times.

M.P., 126

Neurosis is the common disease of every man who has no hope except in himself. Being "fed up" with life, he becomes cynical, self-centered, asserts himself in loud, boorish, boasting tones to atone for his own inner hunger, nakedness and ignorance.

P.R., 201

The New Order

The birth of the Son of God in the flesh was the introduction into the historical world-order of a new life; it was a proclamation to the world that social reconstruction has something to do with spiritual regeneration; that nations can be saved only by the men in them being re-born to God as God is now being born to man.

P., 7

New York *Times*

Mankind wants to hear what God says, not the New York *Times*.

M.P., 87

Criticism derives its attention from the dignity of the one attacked; for example, the Church or the bishop or the Pope. An attack on the Pope would get the first page in the New York *Times* any Monday morning.

M.P., 254

Newscaster

Not trained in memorizing either facts or ideas, it is now almost impossible for the modern man to make an announcement on the radio or television without reading from notes.

W.I., 125

Newspaper

. . . nothing is as old as yesterday's newspaper.

O.B., 287

The art of speech has been studied with great competency from Aristotle onward, but few there are who regard the morals of speech. If a moral man sat down to decide for himself the one secular profession he would approach with the greatest reluctance, because of the responsibility it involved, that profession would be the publishing of a newspaper. An unskilled doctor could kill the body, but he who would use the printed word either to kill a soul, or deprive it of a single grain of divine truth, or put into it a single germ of evil would be guilty of the greater crime.

W.I., 130

Nietzsche, Friedrich Wilhelm

He said that if one did not accept Christ one ought to go crazy, which he did.

L.4, 206

Nihilism and Spirituality

. . . those who refuse to take seriously any moral or spiritual question end by taking Nothingness seriously, which is the area of the eternal subterranean. But if we take the soul seriously, then we are able to take everything else rather lightly.

W.H., 38

Noble

There are very few who have to take a prominent place in the great conflicts of our age; the vast majority must dwell in humbler scenes and be content to do a more humble work. The conflicts which a man has to endure either against evil in his own soul or in the moral circle where his influence would seem to be trivial are in reality the struggle of the battle for life and decency; and true heroism is shown here as well as in those grander scales in which others win the leader's fame or the martyr's crown. Little duties carefully discharged; little temptations earnestly resisted with the strength which God supplies; little sins crucified; these all together help to form that character which is to be described not as popular or glamorous, but as moral and noble.

W.I., 16

O

Obedience

There is no obedience worth anything which is not the child of love. Obedience which is mechanical and forced is dread.

O.B., 169

Obedience in the home is the foundation of obedience in the commonwealth, for in each instance conscience submits to a trustee of God's authority.

O.B., 174

Obedience is servility only to those who have not understood the spontaneity of love.

W.L., 85

Obscurity

Obscurity is a menace only to those who want the plaudits of men.

L.2, 75

Old and Young

It is very easy for young men to see visions and to have the forward look in time; but to the old on whom the sun is casting a forward shadow, it is not easy to dream dreams.

D.L., 81–82

Old as "New"

Some things are "new" to people only because they do not know what is old. It is conceivable that the best ideas may be those that resist the moods and fashions of the time: dead bodies float downstream; it is only live bodies that go against the current.

L.2, 40

Omission

Sins of omission have their penalties as well as sins of commission. There is a penalty for not sowing, just as there is a penalty for sowing thistles. Man loses his character not only because of the evil he does, but also because of the good he leaves undone.

D.L., 68

Ontological Tension

There is not a single error of history which is not a perversion of this mysterious body-soul unity. Some considered the body impure, such as the Manicheans; some considered the soul a parasite or a myth, such as Freud or Nietzsche. Everyone must decide for himself how this pull of opposites is to be resolved. There are only two answers possible: one is to give primacy to the body, in which case the soul suffers; the other is to give primacy to the soul, in which case the body is disciplined.

T.M., 47

The Open-minded

. . . they are willing to hear all sides, but refuse to accept any. Their minds are so "open" that ideas pass right through. It is to be remembered that the "open mind" is no more important than the open mouth. Unless the mouth shuts on something, the body is never nourished. Unless the mind shuts on truth, it is never at peace.

T.T., 3

Open-mindedness

The Moderns are those who believe in moderation. They hate excesses either good or evil; compromise is the very essence of life; they have an "open mind"—in fact so open that they never close it on anything absolutely right and true; they are what the Scriptures call "luke-warm," but they prefer to call themselves "broad."

S.C., 83

"Opium of the People"

No! Religion is not the opium of the people. Opium is the drug of deserters who are afraid to face the Cross—the opiate that gives momentary escape from the Hound of Heaven in pursuit of the human soul.

R.S., 78

Order (Social)

We will never have social order by inciting Capital and Labor to violence, any more than we will have domestic peace by arming wives with rolling pins to knock all affection out of their husbands' heads.

L.E., 53

A true social order can be built only on the basis of fraternity; namely, one inspired not by profit motive, which is capitalism; not by the political motive which is Fascism; not by the violence motive which is Communism, but by the love motive which is Christianity. Start with fraternity, which means that all men are brothers under the Fatherhood of God, that all must function for the common good of society and for the peace of the world, and liberty and equality will follow.

L.E., 83

The Ordinary

When we rest on the laurels of the ordinary, we clip the wings of charity.

L.A., 111

Original Sin

Original sin does not mean that we are born in the state we are in, but that through Adam we have fallen into that state.

P.R., 53

Original sin, it has been said, is something like a severe illness which has upset our nature, with the result that there is a civil war going on inside us, our body rebelling against our soul, because our soul rebelled against God. Just as one country will sometimes "break off relations" with another country, so man by sin became separated from God and lost the gift by which he could attain his true supernatural end.

P.R., 98–99

The Overprivileged

Western civilization proves it is the overprivileged rather than the underprivileged who are suffering from mental breakdowns.

L.4, 247

P

Pacifism

The pacifist thinks that the alternative to war is peace; it is not. Sometimes the alternative is oppression. Sometimes certain God-given rights and liberties can be preserved only by resistance to that which would destroy them. And to defend certain basic God-given rights and liberties is not immoral but righteous.

D.D., 60

Pagan

The pagan fears the loss of his body and his wealth; the faithful fears the loss of his soul.

P.S., 195

Paganism (Modern)

The difference between the paganism of Hitler and the paganism of much of the rest of the world, is a difference only of degree, not of kind; of quantity, not of quality. Note that we are comparing paganisms, nothing else. What Hitler hands out in concentrated form, we in America sell piecemeal; what Hitler sells wholesale, we sell retail. . . .

Paganism and idolatry and alienation from God have reached full bloom, blossom, and fruit in Germany, but in America the seed has been planted.

D.D., 107

New Paganism may be defined as an outlook on life that holds to the sufficiency of human science without faith, and the sufficiency of human power without grace. In other words, its two tenets are: Scientism, which is a deification of the experimental method, and Humanism, which is a glorification of a man who makes God to his own image and likeness.

O.E., 325

Pain

When pain is divorced from love, it leads a man to wish others were as he is; it makes him cruel, hateful, bitter. When pain is unsanctified by affection, it scars, burns up all our finer sensibilities of the soul, and leaves the soul fierce and brutal. Pain as pain, then, is not an ideal: it is a curse, when separated from love, for rather than making one's soul better, it makes it worse by scorching it.

E.G., 215

. . . the great tragedy of the world is not what people suffer, but how much they miss when they suffer. Nothing is quite as depressing as wasted pain, agony without an ultimate meaning or purpose.

O.B., 53

Pain in itself is not unbearable; it is the failure to understand its meaning that is unbearable. If that thief did not see purpose in pain he would never have saved his soul. Pain can be the death of our soul, or it can be its life.

R.S., 26

Parable

The serious can never speak in parables, because the parables are for only those with a sense of the invisible.

M.T., 70

Parasite

To learn without study, to get paid without working, to enjoy a reputation without earning it, to enjoy peace without practicing justice is to cheat both nature and reason. Inanimate nature has its parasites, but for man to be a parasite is to invite his destruction.

D.L., 67

Parents

There are problem children only because there are problem parents.

S.P., 82

There is a bewildering and a personal humiliation on discovering that [one's] father is just like any other father and [one's] mother is just like any other mother.

T.T., 157

Passions

Indifference kills passions; while scepticism deadens them.

W.I., 73

. . . the root of all passions are love and its opposite hate. Hence our passions are either for the pursuit of what we love, or escape from what we hate.

W.I., 73

The Past

Today is but the product of all our yesterdays, and our present is but the harvest of the past.

W.I., 163

Patience

In every direction the great is reached through the little.

W.I., 17

Patience is not something one is born with; it is something that is achieved, such as seeing.

W.I., 134

There are many who excuse themselves, saying that if they were in other circumstances they would be much more patient. This is a grave mistake, for it assumes that virtue is a matter of geography, and not of moral effort. It makes little difference where we are; it all depends on what we are thinking about.

W.I., 135

Patience is power.

W.I., 136

Patriotism

Patriotism is a form of piety. And there are three principle forms of piety love of God, love of neighbor, and love of country. All three are grounded in justice.

S.P., 72

Peace

Peace is the tranquillity of order—not tranquillity alone, because robbers can be tranquil in the possession of their spoils. The sea is tranquil very often before a storm. Peace is the tranquillity of order, and order implies justice, and justice implies law. There is peace in an individual when there is subordination of senses to reason, of reason to faith, of body to soul, of the whole personality to God.

L.I, 244

Peace (Christian)

Peace for us means a right conscience, not a dictatorship over the proletariat . . . not the overthrow of society; it means loving our enemies, not despising them; it means something in the inside of a man's soul, not something outside like a sickle and a hammer.

C.B., 95

Peace (Communist)

For the Communists there can be no real peace until there has been a complete destruction of all private property, the abolition of morals and religion, the subjection of all democratic processes to a totalitarian dictator. That is the goal; but the tactic is to talk peace in order to induce nations to disarm and to convince them that the Moscow-inspired revolutions are purely local. By these ruses they hope to demoralize the rest of the world and prepare for its ultimate conquest.

L.I, 244

Peace of Soul

Psychiatry is able to give a certain measure of peace of mind, for it adjusts the mind to the mood and temper of the world; but it never inquires whether we *ought* to adjust ourselves so completely to the present society. . . . Peace of *soul* is a different and a finer thing; it results from justice, not from adjustment, from rebirth, not from integration to the values of the moment. *Pax opus justitiae.*

P.S., 231

Here is a psychological suggestion for acquiring peace of soul. Never brag; never talk about yourself; never rush to first seats at table or in a theatre; never use people for your own advantage; never lord it over others as if you were better than they.

W.I., 11

Peace (World)

World peace can be recovered only by a spiritual force which avoids the two extremes of Individualism and Communism; a force which asserts against Individualism that man cannot live apart from society; and one which equally asserts against Communism that a person has rights to worship God which the State cannot take away.

P., 28

Peasant versus Worker

The factory worker with all his boasted "social security" is fundamentally insecure. He works on someone else's property, uses someone else's tools, procures increased purchasing power through becoming depersonalized, in a mass movement, and in the end has nothing to pass on to his children. The man with a little bit of land is the stable element in society; he is his own boss, has the joy of seeing a seed planted by his own hands grow to fruit, and above all has that sanity and peace that come from being able to put his hands into God's own earth.

O.B., 135

Pelagianism and Secular Humanism

What was Pelagianism? It was a doctrine taught by a great student of Greek philosophy, Pelagius by name, who held that human nature by its own power is able to save itself without the help of God's grace. This is the central doctrine of Humanism. Note the parallel between the two. Both deny original sin, but both admit the conflict of matter and spirit as a psychological factor; both deny that it is necessary to have recourse to the grace of Christ, though admitting the beauty of Christ; finally, both appeal to the will of man as sufficient to save without the new motive force of grace, which makes man a child of God rather than a creature.

O.E., 217

Penance

One reason for a long life is penance. Time is given us not just to accumulate that which we cannot take with us, but to make reparation for our sins.

R.S., 7

There is a marvelous peace that comes into the soul if all trials and disappointments, sorrows and pains are accepted either as a deserved chastisement for our sins, or as a healthful discipline which will lead us to greater virtue.

W.I., 26

People

The nice people judge themselves by the vices from which they abstain; the awful people judge themselves by the virtues from which they have fallen.

L.2, 112

People (Modern)

Too many people get credit for being good, when they are only passive. They are too often praised for being broadminded when they are so broadminded they can never make up their minds about anything.

S.C., 93

People ("Nice")

The Cross of Calvary stands at the crossroads of three prosperous civilizations as eloquent testimony to the uncomfortable truth that the successful people, the social leaders, the people who are labeled *nice* are the ones most capable of crucifying the Divine Truth and the Eternal Love.

P.S., 69

Persecution

A Jew knows that today all religions are persecuted. No race and no faith has a monopoly on persecution. Protestants have been persecuted in Germany, and Catholics, like the Jews, have been persecuted in every age.

L.A., 132–133

Why do we pick and choose among barbarities? Is killing in a beer hall wrong and persecution in a sanctuary pardonable?
   The Catholic who condemns the persecution of the Protestants in Germany but not the persecution of the Jews, has no right to his protest any more than the Jew who condemns persecution of his countrymen in Germany, but ignores the persecution of Protestants in Germany, or Catholics in Mexico . . . choosing among barbarities will simply mean the advent of *our* form of barbarism.

W.W., 17–18

Person

Individuals are replaceable; persons are irreplaceable and unique.

O.B., 137

• 225 •

Person and Rights

A person is a being with a rational soul and, therefore, has rights.
A pig has no rational soul and, therefore, has no rights. . . . A
baby has a soul and, therefore, has inalienable rights, even though
the baby cannot express its desire to live. Rights do not depend on
utility or social welfare, but on the soul itself. Abortion is wrong
because if the soul is there, there is a person.

L.I, 212–213

Person (Sanctity of)

The Saviour said that each one of us is of more worth than the
whole visible universe!

W.I., 50

Person versus Humanity

Humanity is indeed sacred, but those who glorified humanity often
used it as a cloak for the gravest injustices and cruelties to certain
humans. A Dostoevski character said that he loved mankind in
general and could give learned discourses on the necessity of loving
mankind, but that if he were left in a room half a day with a man
who had a peculiar way of blowing his nose, he began to despise
him. Humanity was loved but not always the human. Rousseau,
who glorified humanity in his politics, also deserted each of his
children immediately after birth.

O.B., 135

Personality

Free choice is the essence of personality.

O.B., 160

Perfection of personality does not consist in knowing God's plan, but in submitting to it as it reveals itself in the circumstances of life.

S.W., 32

Personhood

The most fundamental difference between Christianity and Marxism is in their respective concepts of the value of the individual person. The idea of the sacredness of human personality is inseparable from Christianity; but it is an obstacle to Marxism, which declares that the individual finds his perfection only in a class.

P.O., 265

In each of us there are several persons: there is the person others think you are; there is the person *you* think you are; there is the person you *really are*.

P.R., 132

Pessimism

The fruit of pessimism blossom on the tree of a dissolute life.

S.V., 38

Pessimist

Every pessimist is a frustrated hedonist!

W.H., 28

Philosophers

There are as many Gods as there are philosophers.

G.I., 196

Philosopher (Modern)

Those who have most contributed to philosophical chaos are now assuming a pessimistic outlook for the philosophical future which they have helped to create.

G.I., 5

I am the absolute; my neighbor is hell. A German philosopher in the same spirit of egotism said that if it could be mathematically proved and with absolute certitude that God exists I would still reject His existence because He would set a limit to my ego. "Thy will be done" becomes "my will be done."

L.4, 46

If men want ghosts, the democratic philosophers, who know the will of the populace, will write a philosophy justifying ghosts; if the man in the street wants to follow the line of least moral resistance, philosophers will develop for him the justifying philosophy of "self-expression"; if the man of affairs has no time for the thoughts of eternity, then philosophers develop for him the philosophy of "space-time."

O.E., 44

Philosopher's Life

What is true in the moral order is true in the speculative order. There is often a wide breach between what a philosopher teaches and the principles upon which he acts in his ordinary life.

G.I., 142

Philosophy

Philosophy satisfies only for a time, but it leaves so little to love.

D.L., 160

Philosophical errors are reducible in principle to exaggeration or defect.

G.I., 146

Philosophy and Fads

The philosopher who knows the method and content and principles of his science will . . . not become excited when a new physical theory is offered to the world. Hence, we have little sympathy for those philosophers who, forgetting the principles which gave them certitude within their field, feel that the Quantum Theory proves free-will, or that there is a God because the physics of Eddington and Jeans say there is a God. The Quantum Theory has nothing more to do with the proof of free-will than a proton has to do with a wish to be moral. The existence of God did not wait for Eddington and Jeans, and those fundamentalists who enthused about science becoming theistic are very apt to find their theism overthrown when the theories of these two notable scientists are upset. The life of a physical theory today has only about the life of a peace treaty.

PH., 182

Philosophy and Science

The method of physics is not the method of sociology nor is the method of chemistry the method of religion. Neither are the objects of any of these sciences the same, otherwise there would be no distinction of sciences. This being so, *it is a fallacy to suppose that philosophy should change* its principles with every new advance in biology, psychology, chemistry, or physics. There are fads in science, just as there are fads in clothes, and during the past few generations these fads have been sociology, biology, psychology, and physics.

PH., 180

Physics, biology, and sociology are not the ground and foundation of metaphysics; otherwise the science with a more restricted object would rule the science with a more general object. That is why St. Thomas asserts that a changed conception of empirical science does not involve a change in the metaphysics which ruled that science.

R.G., 246

Philosophy (Modern)

It may even be added that modern philosophy in recent years has been playing so fast and loose with common sense, "believing what no one else ever believed before," that the time will soon come when a modern philosopher who returns to common sense will be hailed as one of the most original thinkers of all time.

G.I., 146

The Absolutist denied morality to God to save His absoluteness; the Pragmatist denied absoluteness to save His morality; and the biological philosopher makes the supreme renunciation: He gives up God to save man.

G.I., 265–266

Such is the spirit of modern philosophy—divinization of man and humanization of God.

G.I., 285

Philosophy . . . has become so obsessed with that notion that it teaches with unbuttoned pride that there is no such thing as Truth with a capital "T," for Truth is ambulatory: we make it as we go; it depends on the Time in which we live.

M.T., 226

Philosophy of Life

There is a world of difference between a mind that has in it ten thousand bits of uncorrelated information, and a mind that is like an organism in which one fact or truth is functionally related to every other truth, as the heart is related to the legs and arms. The wisest of men reads out of a philosophy of life, as he eats out of a philosophy of health.

W.I., 108

Physician (Modern)

He wants that type of killing legalized so that it will not be the "I," but "they," or the law, who is responsible. The very search for legality is in itself a recognition of the crime of murder, which one seeks to escape by throwing the burdens on the anonymous or the state. Such men with criminal intent think that by making the handle of the knife long enough, or by putting it into the hands of the state, they will make murder legal.

L.2, 37

Pilate

To have some idea of Pilate's personality and his vision of the world worldly, make a mental picture of him in terms of one of our modern intelligentsia—a reader of Mencken, Bertrand Russell, and Shaw, with Swinburne and Wells on his bookshelves, one whose emotional life was dictated by Havelock Ellis and his mental life by Julian Huxley, who says there is no such thing as truth.

E.G., 119

Pilgrimage

To live by the day and to watch each step is the true pilgrimage method, for there is nothing little if God requires it.

W.I., 18

Pity versus Compassion

Pity is an aristocratic virtue; it looks down on the suffering of others. Compassion is the democratic virtue; it shares suffering and pain and feels it as its own.

L.2, 32

Platitudes

Platitudes belong only to those who say we must have new morals to suit the new science. Platitudes are the heritage of time, but not of the eternal.

E.G., 105

Plato

. . . Plato, who argues that love is the first step toward religion. He pictures love for beautiful persons being transformed into love for beautiful souls, then into a love of justice, goodness, and God, Who is their source.

T.M., 50

Play

Play is unlike work because it lacks the high seriousness of work, or a purpose, or an end. Play is an end in itself; work is for something else.

L.4, 55

Pleasure

A law deeply graven on every human heart is: the more we give way to pleasures, the more we diminish the pleasure.

D.L., 34

Pleasure is like beauty; it is conditioned by contrast.

W.H., 48

Pleasure is very peculiar: to possess it one must not seek it directly, but rather seek it through something else.

W.I., 153

Our complex modern society is directed to the creation of mass pleasure rather than individual pleasure. Movies, television, advertising are geared to the masses, and generally to their lowest common denominator. Their aim is to satisfy what men have in common, rather than what they have individually.

W.I., 153

Pleasure versus Joy

Pleasure is associated with the body: for instance, we feel pleasure after a good meal. Joy is of the heart, and it comes from a good conscience. Joy hears music on the inside even when discords are ringing outside. Pleasure depends on outward circumstances, for example, wealth, friends, and wine, and therefore it can be obliterated by the slightest toothache. Joy is independent of outward circumstances; it can be felt even in adversity and pain.

L. 5, 193

Poet

Poets are those who have been richly endowed with a sense of the invisible, who can look out upon exactly the same phenomena that other mortals take seriously, and see in them something of the Divine.

M.T., 71

Poland

The last World War started because of Poland. Its modern history has been that of a crucifixion between two thieves—Nazism and Communism. Nothing will happen to the world until something happens to Poland.

O.B., 276

Poland is the cameo of the world situation; the knot of political Europe; the key to whether we will have justice or force in the world for the next hundred years.

O.B., 288

Political Health

The political health of any nation can be measured by how much the people expect the state to give them and how little they expect to do for themselves, or how much they believe the world owes them a living.

O.B., 262

Political Power

The question of Pilate was that of all dictators who presume that the power of government is final and absolute. Our Lord reads to the arrogant Roman the lesson which he and all of his tribe in all ages and in all lands need—that their power is derived from God, therefore it is in its foundation legitimate, and in its exercise it is to be guided by His will and used for His purposes.

T.T., 202

Politician

By "politicians" we mean statesmen who have become victims of expediency, dupes of opportunism and Simple Simons of pragmatism.

D.L., 84

A dishonest politician will invariably accuse all politicians of being dishonest.

L.A., 116

When a politician boasts that he loves the poor, find out how much of his capital he has given to the poor.

O.B., 131

A moment may come in the life of a politician, for example, when, in order to keep his independence, he must sacrifice the ease and influence which comes with the bribe.

R.S., 97

Some day a politician will arise who will be so devoted to truth that he will follow it, knowing that by doing so, he will go down to defeat. That day will be the restoration of politics as principles; it will also be the rebirth of a nation.

W.I., 68

Politics

Marxism held that "religion is the opium of the people." Today this may mean politics is the heroin of religion.

M.P., 14

The Church has always taught that one form of government is not absolutely better than any other form of government, so long as the person is recognized as superior to the State.

S.P., 65

Politics has become so primary in modern life, that the masses are more moved by promises than by fulfillments.

W.I., 68

Politics and Economics

Both economics and politics are doomed to unreality and failure unless grounded on the recognition that man is a spiritual being with ideals beyond this world. To recommend only political and economic panaceas for the world problem of dehumanized forgotten man, is like recommending face powder for someone suffering from jaundice, or an alcohol rub for someone suffering from cancer.

P., 39

Politics as the New Theology

Social conscience takes the place of individual conscience. That is why the followers of the new demonic mysticism feel that by blaming others they relieve themselves of blame; by liquidating certain persons guilty of injustice, they dispense themselves from the guilt of their own personal injustices. That too is why in all totalitarianism there goes hand in hand a great passion for social reform with a complete disinterest in the need of individual reform. By lifting the beam out of their neighbor's eyes, they need not be concerned with the mote in their own. Politics then becomes the new theology.

C.C., 171

Politics (Modern)

Our Constitution puts politics under theology, democracy under God. But today, politics denies its divine foundation. Politics is today the supreme and absolute science. We once lived in the age of the Theological Man; then came the age of the Economic Man; now we are in the age of Political Man. The Theological Man lived for God; the Economic Man lived for profit; the Political Man lives for the State.

S.P., 63

What economics was to the days of Liberalism, politics is to the Modern Man. So important has politics become, that now men judge religion by its attitude toward politics, rather than politics by its attitude toward religion.

S.P., 64

The Poor

Some poor hate the rich not because they have unjustly stolen their possessions, but because *they* want their possessions. Certain *have-nots* are scandalized at the wealth of the *haves,* only because they are tempted by lust for their possessions.

V.V., 16

The Poor in Spirit

The poor in spirit are those who are so detached from wealth, from social position, and from earthly knowledge that, at the moment the Kingdom of God demands a sacrifice, they are prepared to surrender all.

C.B., 54

Possession

Possession dulls.

F.D., 30

Possessions

There is a profound difference in quality between the possessions that we need, and use, and actually enjoy, and the accumulation of useless things we accumulate out of vanity or greed or the desire to surpass others.

W.H., 45

Poverty

Poverty is a peril and a disgrace only to those who want to be rich.

L.2, 75

We can eliminate immediately the antiquated idea that poverty is the cause of inner disharmony—for if that were so, all the rich would be normal.

P.S., 32

Power

The more *real* power a person has, the less boasting is needed.

T.T., 12

Power and Wealth

No man has a right to power until he has learned obedience, as Christ was obedient to His parents. And no man may safely possess wealth until he has learned to be detached from it.

W.H., 109

The Powerful

The powerful are always under obligation to the weak. Advantage of any kind is not a personal possession but a trust.

O.B., 128

Pragmatism

What is useful is true, according to Pragmatism. If God is useful for your life, He exists for you; if He is not useful for my life, He does not exist for me. The individual is all-important. Pragmatism was a war against Truth. Truth is not transcendental, it declared; it is ambulatory. It is personal and individual.

O.E., 122

Pragmatism is the logical consequence of a denial of the objectivity of truth. It may glory in the fact that as an epistemology it can be said to correspond to human needs, yet it still remains true that one of the greatest of human needs is to be something more than a pragmatist.

R.G., 293

Pragmatist

The most popular form of covering up hatred of Truth and fear of Goodness is indifference, which the intelligentsia . . . call agnosticism; they deny that Truth exists. By a cultivated indifference to the distinction between truth and error, they hope to render themselves immune from any responsibility for the way they live. But the studied refusal to distinguish between right and wrong is not, in fact, indifference, or neutrality—it is an acceptance of the wrong. Pilate, the first pragmatist, sneered, "What is Truth?" and after doing so, he crucified It.

L.H., 23

Praise

One test of true humility is our attitude towards praise. Anyone who loves publicity is proud, is seeking to be justified before men; for the humble man refers all praise to God.

W.H., 21

Praise is given to strangers frequently, but less to those of our own household.

W.I., 40

Praise and Gossip

The world is either saying things about us that are too good to be true, or too bad to be true.

D.L., 15

Prayer

Prayer is helplessness casting itself on Power, infirmity leaning on Strength, misery reaching to Mercy, and a prisoner clamoring for Relief.

L.2, 213

. . . there are not two kinds of answers to prayer, but three: One is "Yes." Another is "No." The third is "Wait."

S.W., 60

Preacher

The preacher who bores others in the pulpit is a bore before he ever gets into it. He is not in love. He is not on fire with Christ. He is a burned out cinder floating in the immensity of catchwords. "For the words that the mouth utters come from the overflowing of the heart" (Luke 6:45). Some other source than Christ is behind the sociological platitudes, moral chestnuts and political bromides of the preacher.

M.P., 88

Preacher (Modern)

Many a modern preacher is far less concerned with preaching Christ and Him crucified than he is with his popularity with his congregation.

O.E., 100

Preaching

It is Christ the people want to hear about, not boycotts, stocks, marches, protests. They have their place, but not as a substitute for Christ. The Jesus people arose to fill a lacuna of the pulpits.

M.P., 86

Prejudice

Knowledge of the moral life is conditioned upon the removal of all prejudice.

M.U., 2

Preppies

They send their children to the best schools they can afford; never send them to church, but let them go to the movies at least twice a week; they take their politics from a radio commentator; their economics from their son who has had one year of it under a Marxist Professor in College. They think there are too many divorces, but after all we are not living in the Middle Ages; they believe that the majority is always right; that religion does add some sentiment and symbolism to life—in a word, they are what their neighbors would call "good" people.

S.C., 84

"Presence of God"

"Presence of God" is a phrase very loosely used today to cover anything from the Pantheism of the Lake poets to the vague sentimentalism of the Romanticist, who likes the woods because he "feels" God there. God is, indeed, present in the universe in many various ways. . . . But a far more intimate presence was evidenced in the Incarnation, where God appeared as man in the heart of a new humanity which was to become His new Body.

P.S., 245–246

The Press

Not long ago one of the nationally known picture magazines had a photograph of a man prostrate on subway stairs. For thirty minutes many people passed him by without ever a helping hand. The editorial comment was about the coldness of the modern man in the face of distress. What was forgotten was that the photographer of the picture magazine did nothing for thirty minutes for the afflicted individual except to snap pictures and make his own living.

O.B., 274

Pride

There is no better way to keep God out of your soul than to be full of self.

L.A., 45

Every proud person takes himself too seriously.

L.A., 83

Pride manifests itself in many forms: *atheism,* which is a denial of our dependence on God, our Creator and our final end; *intellectual vanity,* which makes minds unteachable because they think they know all there is to know; *superficiality,* which judges others by their clothes, their accent, and their bank account; *snobbery,* which sneers at inferiors as the earmark of its own superiority.

V.V., 42

Pride slays thanksgiving.

W.H., 192

It is a spiritual and a psychological fact that some people who pride themselves on their virtue resent sinners mending their ways.

W.I., 39

Pride rightly has been called the source of all other evils.

W.I., 119

Pride versus Humility

Since pride is a capital sin, it follows that a first condition of conversion is humility: the ego must decrease, God must increase. This humiliation most often comes by a profound realization that sin does not pay, that it never keeps its promises, that just as a violation of the laws of health produces sickness, so the violation of the laws of God produces unhappiness.

C.P., 9

Pride is the child of ignorance, humility the offspring of knowledge.

W.I., 11

Priest

Each priest is a man with a body of soft clay. To keep that treasure pure, he has to be stretched out on a cross of fire. Our fall can be greater than the fall of anyone else because of the height from which we tumble. Of all the bad men, bad religious men are the worst, because they were called to be closer to Christ.

A., 4

A priest is one who makes Christ visible. The people see Christ in the saintly priest and they seek even to touch his robes as they did the robe of Christ. Children come to him without fear; non-Catholics give to them a reverence which they rarely give to others. The measure by which a priest draws souls to Christ is also the measure by which he can drive souls from Christ.

M.P., 218

It has been said of priests that, if they shoot golf under 80, there is something wrong with their priesthood; if they shoot golf over 80, there is something wrong with their golf.

T.T., 143

Priest (Revolutionary)

Much more interested in politics, banners, protests, international strife, than in his theology and parish. Defends guerrilla warfare in any nation where it erupts. Particularly bitter against any priest who makes his peace with any given political situation.

M.P., 191–192

Priest-Counselor

From a theological point of view, every sick person has his cross, and this is the way the priest-counselor sees patients on their special Calvaries.

M.P., 78

Procrastination

The road to Hell is paved with stones of *postponed* resolutions.

O.B., 324

God has promised men pardon if they are penitent, but not if they procrastinate.

P.S., 177

Procreation

Nothing is more binding than a child, who is the symbol of the survival of man, the pledge of the resurrection of the body. . . . Nothing is more religious in nature than procreation; it is the sign both of unity and continuity.

T.M., 194

Products (Modern)

It has reached a point now in the prosperity of our civilization where it is almost impossible to get a thing repaired. When one brings an auto, a radio, a television set, a toaster, or a carpet sweeper to be repaired, the usual retort is, "Throw it away; buy a new one." Be discontented with anything but "next year's model."

O.B., 89

Professionalism

. . . love is the condition of service. Professionalism is service
without love.

F.D., 96

Progress

Since the world accepted Rousseau's thesis of the natural goodness
of man without God, there have been six major wars, and four
supreme revolutions. Between the Napoleonic wars and the
Franco-Prussian War there intervened fifty-five years; between the
Franco-Prussian War and the first World War, forty-three years; between the last World War and this war, twenty-one years. Fifty-five,
forty-three, twenty-one—and each succeeding war more destructive
than the last, not only of life and property, but of truth, liberty,
and belief in God. Do our progressive friends call that "Progress"?

D.D., 25

The word "progress," which means an approach toward an ideal,
now means the changing of the ideal. A man was said to be making
"progress" in driving to Washington from New York when he got
as far as Philadelphia; now he is said to make "progress" when he
ends up in Portland, Maine.

D.L., 137

Progress is necessarily conservative. To perfect we must conserve
the gains of the past.

G.I., 268

A Catholic believes that the only true progress in the world consists in the diminution of the traces of original sin.

L.A., 50

Progress in an indefinite future, but not beyond history, makes present moral lives meaningless and endows them with no other value than that of so many sticks to keep the cosmic bonfire blazing for the next generation. When the only kind of happiness men can enjoy is one which they celebrate in the distant future on the graves of their ancestors, then indeed their happiness is the happiness of grave diggers in the midst of a pestilence.

P.W., 43

. . . history does not prove we are making progress; instead of evolving from savagery to civilization, we seem to be devolving from civilization to savagery.

P.W., 48

The one thing in the world that never progresses is the idea of progress.

R.G., 220

Progressives

This group has led parents to believe that evil, sin and crime are due to ignorance, and that if we educate by imparting knowledge we will abolish crime. Typical of this was Guizot, who when non-religious education began said: "He who opens a school, closes a prison." Today the facts retort to Guizot: "Well, we opened thousands of schools, but we closed no prisons."

S.P., 81

They measure progress by the height of the pile of discarded moral truths.

S.W., 83

He is going nowhere but he is sure he is on the way.

W.H., 165

Without ever saying so, they assume that man is responsible for everything good and beautiful in the world, but God is responsible for its wickedness and its wars.

W.W., 39

Propaganda

The unfortunate characteristic of our day is that propaganda has taken the place of personal influence.

W.I., 68

Property

Property . . . is the economic guarantee of human liberty, the external manifestation of inner responsibility. Deprive man of the right to fashion things according to his own will, and you deprive him, at one stroke, of the social basis of his freedom.

F.G., 212

This soul infused by God is the source of his rights. Because he is dependent on God, he is independent of an absolute state. But man must have some guarantee on the *outside* that he is free. That guarantee is property.

O.B., 135

. . . to *have* is the legitimate extension of . . . *being.*

Wherever property is, there is power.

Property (Communizing)

Communizing property does not do away with social injustice; it only transfers opportunities for its debasement into fewer hands.

Prophet

A prophet is a *Divine Troubler,* not a political troubler. He is always a disturber of worldly peace; he makes listeners feel uneasy. As the world settles into mediocrity, there is a tendency to judge oneself by his peers; the younger by the young, the old by the old. Too many clubs of mutual exoneration exist in the world today.

Prostitution

The difference between prostitution and love is that in the former there is the offering of the body without the soul. True love demands that the will to love should precede the act of possession.

The Proud

The proud seek only to make others acknowledge them as gods and goddesses.

W.H., 106–107

Psychoanalysis

There are thousands of patients on their backs who would be made better today if they were on their knees instead.

P.S., 89

. . . the psychoanalytic method is a substitute for confession.

P.S., 112

Psychoanalysis versus Confession

It costs considerable money to tell one's complexes to a psychoanalyst; it costs only pride and arrogance of soul to confess our sins to representatives of the moral and Divine order.

G.T., 118

Psychologism

Psychologism denies that defeat, frustration, trials, discouragement, and suffering are the make-up of life.

D.L., 149

Psychologist

. . . who has established the analyst as a prototype for any man to take as normal?

P.S., 128

Psychologist (Modern)

Anyone who has read hundreds of works on modern psychology has been struck by the fact that practically all agree that a man does not know what is going on inside his own mind.

D.L., 150

Such . . . analysts tell the client, at one moment, that he was determined to be the way he is by infantile urgings or by the herd instinct, so that he is not responsible for his wrong; the next moment, they tell him that he is now responsible for his future condition.

P.S., 128

Psychology

Modern psychology which explains the tension between the lower and the higher self, between man and his environment, is but a psychological description of the fall of man.

E.I., 77

Psychiatrists occasionally fill the void created by the want of genuine concern for the ills and woes of people on the part of the clergy. The state has largely taken over education; now psychology would take the soul away from the priest.

P.N., 142

Psychology (Dehumanizing)

. . . a psychology which denies the human soul is constantly contradicting itself. It calls man an animal and then proceeds to describe a human anxiety which is never found in any animal devoid of a rational soul.

P.S., 18

Psychology (Modern)

Psychology . . . first said that man had no soul, then that he had no mind, and finally no conscience. The truly psychological was explained by the physiological, and man who was once defined as a rational animal was now reduced to the state of a physiological machine which behaved in response to the physical law of action and reaction.

C.C., 63

Some one once told the story of a man who went out from England in a row-boat, came back, and made a great discovery—he discovered England. It is not unlikely that in the near future, the psychologists who left the shores of sane thinking in the row-boat *Novelty* will soon come back to those shores once again, and will make a great discovery—they will discover a soul. And those who make that discovery will be hailed as original thinkers, for if error multiplies, the most novel and original thing in the world will be truth.

O.E., 209

Psychology (Social)

It is interesting how a materialistic civilization describes the rich as suffering from an "anxiety neurosis," and the poor as being plain "nuts" or "crackpots."

T.M., 61

Psychotherapy

Every normal person if he is interested in the development of his character along the lines of moral rectitude will gain more by five minutes on his knees than he will in sixty hours on a couch—and it is much cheaper, too.

L.4, 12

Psychotics and Neurotics

A psychotic believes that two and two make five; a neurotic believes that two and two make four, but is mad about it. The neurotics hold to the real, and forget the ideal. . . . The psychotics would isolate the Church from the world; the neurotics would identify the Church with the world. For the psychotics, religion is cultic; for the neurotics it is activistic. When Goethe's devil started translating the Gospel of John: "In the beginning was the Word," he hesitated, because he could not subscribe to the primacy of the Word of God. So he wrote instead: "In the beginning was the Deed."

M.P., 19

Public Health (AIDS)

If an epidemic arose in a land, would we say that since people are no longer living according to the laws of hygiene therefore we must revise our hygienic laws to embrace disease, or would we crush the epidemic and retain our faith in health and cleanliness?

C.C., 121

Public Opinion

One of the difficulties in substituting society for God, is that any human society, even at its best, is too often undiscriminating in its judgments, and sometimes too ignorant and cruel, to serve as an object of worship. It likewise fails to take into account the fact that great heroes, saints, and sometimes scholars are those who opposed public opinion in the name of conscience and moral insight. Public opinion and social judgments are sometimes wrong. It was public opinion that crucified Christ.

P.O., 231

Public Speaking

Whenever we hear anyone read a talk, there is always the temptation to ask, "Who wrote it?"

L.2, 62

Much wisdom is hidden in the remark of the old Irishwoman who heard a Bishop reading his discourse. She said . . . "if he can't remember it, how does he expect us to?"

L.2, 62

Publicity

Publicity is artificial stimulation. It is the attribution of worth to those who have either not earned it, or who have no right to it.

P.R., 22

Purgatory

. . . belief in Purgatory has declined in just the proportion that the modern mind forgot the two most important things in the world: the Purity of God and the heinousness of sin.

H.C., 86

Purgatory is that place in which the love of God tempers the justice of God, and secondly, where the love of man tempers the injustice of man.

H.C., 86

Purges

The "purges" of Russia mean that there the right of speech is the right of echo, and then one must fear that the echo is not in keeping with the Party line.

F.G., 190

Purity

Purity . . . is not something negative; it is not just an unopened bud; it is not something cold; it is not ignorance of life. Is justice merely the absence of dishonesty? . . . Is faith merely the absence of doubt? Purity is not merely the absence of sensuality; it is self-lessness born of love and the highest love of all.

C.B., 47

Purity is a reflection of faith; it is attitude before an act; a reverent inwardness, not a biological intactness.

P.N., 257

R

Rape

The enormity of evil associated with rape is precisely because it deprives the woman of making a gift of herself. A quality of immolation or victimhood is, therefore, inherent in woman, though she gets less credit for it.

M.P., 317

Rationalism (Irrational)

Only a century ago Rationalism gloried in having liberated the intelligence from extrinsic control. Now it has denied the rights of reason entirely and falls down before the altar of sentiment. In pulling the mitre from intellectual man it has pulled the head off with it. We are no longer men, but animals. We "feel" our way instead of knowing it.

G.I., 213

Reading

It is not nearly as important to read what is just off the press as it is to read something that needed to be reprinted after a lapse of time.

D.L., 132

While each person is entitled to his preferences, the fact still remains that for the complete development of the mind, there must be serious and intelligent reading—not just reading.

W.I., 107

Reason

Reason was made to lead us to faith as the senses were made to lead us to reason. Now when reason is torn up from its roots in God, how can we trust its conclusions? If chance, blind evolution, or chaos were its origin, then why should it now be expected to be anything less than chaotic, unstable and fluid? An age which has put all its trust in enlightenment as the cure of evil has found itself possessed of the greatest evil and war in the history of the world.

P.W., 74–75

Reason (Loss of)

When Marx makes the ethical and philosophical the unstable superstructure of economic methods of production; when the Freudian tradition makes reason the marionette of the unconscious, and asserts that man's true nature is in the fulfillment of the libido; when sociologists make culture and religion the expression of an environment; when psychology becomes physiology, and physiology, chemistry, so that man is reduced to matter, and therefore a thing—then not only does reason lose its primacy, but man himself has no other value than that of being an instrument of power, political or other.

P.O., xiv

Rebellion

There is not a person in the world who does not feel within himself the triple rebellion which was passed on to us through the rebellion of humanity when it began, namely, lust, or the war of the erotic against the reasonable; pride, or the exaltation of the ego with its contempt of neighbor; or finally, greed, or the inordinate tendency to make character identical with *having* rather than with *being*.

C.I., 69

Reductionism

For the modern sensate mind, to understand is to measure; to know is to count. The senses are the only sources of knowledge.

P.W., 50

The partial views of man as expressed by Marx, Spencer, Darwin and Freud never treat man as he is—really is. These views represent incidental activities erected into absolutes and are of much the same mental construction as would be shown by a dentist who thinks man is all teeth; or a manicurist who thinks he is all hands; or a pedicurist who thinks he is all feet; or a phrenologist who thinks he is all bumps.

P.W., 84

Whenever a new scientific theory is born there are not wanting intelligentsia who set it to music so that every other kind of knowledge in the world dances to its tunes.

W.I., 22

Reformation

In the sixteenth century a reformation was needed. Now there were two reforms possible: one was to reform faith, the other was to reform discipline. The faith was solid; it was the Faith of Christ. The discipline, however, was weak, for it was the discipline of worldliness. The reformers, who sometimes reform the wrong thing, reformed faith instead of discipline, and brought revealed religion to the present state of "confusion worse confounded."

O.E., 82

Reformer

About the only kind of reform one hears of today is social reform. . . . But it must not be forgotten that some people become social reformers in order to escape their own reformation.

D.L. 126

Relativity (Theory of)

There is nothing, of course, in the scientific doctrine of relativity by itself that has any bearing on religion. It is just as indifferent to it as the law of gravitation or the economic law of supply and demand. Relativity of time and space does not mean the relativity of a spatio-temporal religion any more than the imprisoning of ultra-violet rays means an ultra-violet religion. If, therefore, Professor Einstein enunciates a dogma about religion, it is of no more value for religion than the statement of a home-run king about home-brew.

O.E., 257

Religion

Religion is actually not a crutch; it is a cross. It is not an escape, it is a burden; not a flight, but a response. We speak here of a religion with teeth in it, the wind that demands self-sacrifice and surrender. One leans on a crutch, but a cross rests on us. A coward can use a crutch, but it takes a hero to embrace a cross.

D.L., 119

Religion . . . is the elixir which spurs a soul on to the infinite goal for which it was made. Religion supplies the profoundest desires.

R.S., 78

. . . religion is popular only when it ceases to be truly religious. Religion by its very nature is unpopular—certainly unpopular with the ego.

W.I., 92

Religion and Communism

. . . dictatorships, such as the Communistic, regard man only as a stomach to be fed by the State, or as a tool to amass wealth for the State. Put men on that level and they need religion no more than animals need religion. . . . But to put them on that level is to depersonalize and mechanize them down to the very core of their being.

L.E., 134

Religion and Politics

Religion is not to be divorced from public relations, either political or economic, for political and economic actions are human actions, and human actions are moral actions. For that reason the wisest of all pagan writers and the wisest of all Christian thinkers, Aristotle and St. Thomas, housed their treatises of Laws and Politics within the larger library of Ethics. This is as it should be, for political actions and religious actions are subject to the same Eternal Law of God; there is not one law for a politician and another for a saint; Herod the politician will be judged by the same God Who will judge the widow who dropped her mite into the Temple treasury.

W.W., 58–59

Politics exist to lead free men to a prosperous and virtuous common life on this earth; religion exists to save men's souls. But from both of them are born the two greatest loyalties known to man: the cross and the flag.

W.W., 59

Religion and the Secular Order

A religion that does not interfere with the secular order will soon discover that the secular order will not refrain from interfering with it.

F.G., 5

Religion and the State

If by "interference in politics" is meant the interference by the clergy in the political realm of the State, the Church is unalterably opposed to it, for the Church teaches that the State is supreme in the temporal order. But when politics ceases to be politics and begins to be a religion, when it claims supremacy over the soul of man, when it reduces him to a grape for the sake of the wine of collectivity, when it limits his destiny to be a servant of Moloch, when it denies both the freedom of conscience and freedom of religion, when it competes with religion on its own ground, the immortal soul that is destined for God, then religion protests. And when it does, its protest is not against politics but against a counter-religion that is anti-religious.

C.P., 37

Religion as Social

Religion must not only be personal; it must also be social. We do not save ourselves alone, in isolation from others, either politically, economically or religiously. When the enemy of our homes and institutions attacks, we must organize into an army and navy; when the enemy of our souls attacks we must organize into a religious community. Face to face with a world which organizes itself by standards which children of God are bound to repudiate, is it not the business of those children to join themselves together to meet that community of hate by a community of love? If we refuse to seek that unity in God, we will find, as Germany and Russia did, that by excluding God the only unity left is the enforced unity of the army. This is incidentally why the social affirmation of our common fellowship with God is the greatest bulwark of true democracy.

W.W., 53

Religion (Modern)

Modern religion has enunciated one great and fundamental dogma that is at the basis of all the other dogmas, and that is, that religion must be freed from dogmas. Creeds and confessions of faith are no longer the fashion; religious leaders have agreed not to disagree and those beliefs for which some of our ancestors would have died they have melted into a spineless Humanism. Like other Pilates they have turned their backs on the uniqueness of truth and have opened their arms wide to all the moods and fancies the hour might dictate.

O.E., 4–5

The Religious

A great burden is thrust upon men who call themselves religious. In this fatal hour, all of their energies should be spent recalling man to his spiritual destiny. . . . Let those who call themselves Catholics, or Protestants, or Jews recall that the function of their religion is to intensify the spiritual life of man and not to empty the vials of bitterness into hearts, stirring up one against another. It is not to the politicians and the economists and the social reformers that we must look for the first steps in this spiritual recovery; it is to the professed religious.

W.H., 168–169

Religious Beliefs

The great mistake of the nineteenth century was to believe that the intellectual basis of Christian doctrine about God and man, and their mutual relations, could be abolished without in any way impairing morals. Dogmas were considered impossible, but ethics were indispensable; doctrine was ridiculous but morals sublime; the Cross was folly, but the Sermon on the Mount was a masterpiece. Practically all advanced Victorian minds proceeded on the assumption that you could obliterate the religious beliefs of a nation without affecting its moral standards.

C.C., 142

Religious Inspiration

It is therefore not the material and the economic which has failed us, but the moral and religious inspiration to direct our material resources for the common good and the glory of God. This does not mean that there must not be political and economic and financial solutions; but it does mean these are *secondary,* and that they cannot be ultimately attained until we have "entered into ourselves" and discovered the end and purpose of being a man.

P., 38

Religious Persecution

Wicked power cannot stand the vision of an innocent conscience. From the days of youth when the good boy is ridiculed by bad boys, because his goodness is a judgment passed upon them, to the days of maturity when evil men ridicule religion, the moral is ever the same: religious persecution arises in the world not because religion is corrupt, but because consciences are corrupt.

C.P., 56

Persecution is not essentially anti-Semitic, it is not essentially anti-Christian. It is anti-human.

L.A., 133

Remorse

The very feeling following sin, the emptiness which sin engenders, God may use to summon us to be filled with His grace. . . . Sadness, bitterness and cynicism sometimes seize the soul, and with it a fatigue of life. That very emptiness can be the foundation of conversion.

L.A., 49–50

Remorse is the negative presence of God in the soul, as grace is the positive presence of God. Remorse is incomplete, for it is self-disgust divorced from God; but remorse can become sorrow, and then hope, the moment the soul turns to God for help.

L.H., 17

Remorse versus Repentence

Remorse is always a prisoner of the past; it does not shrug its shoulders and forget it. The past is present; the fault is ever before the eyes, but there is no way to undo it. . . .

Repentance is also self-reproach, like the other states, but it is never sterile; it lays hold of the past by undoing it through penance. Both Judas and Peter denied Our Lord, but Judas repented unto himself, which was regret and remorse, and took his own life; Peter repented unto the Lord, which produced a new man.

O.B., 71

Repentance

Repentance is not concerned with consequences. This is what distinguishes it from remorse, which is inspired principally by fear of unpleasant consequences.

P.N., 180

Repose

. . . repose is an activity no less creative than that of our working hours.

Repose—true leisure—cannot be enjoyed without some recognition of the spiritual world. For the first purpose of repose is the contemplation of the good . . . its goal is a true perspective one, the small incidents of everyday life in their relation to the larger goodness that surrounds us.

W.H., 55

Repression

Some "sexiatrists" interpret every dream in terms of sex, thus making it the key to man instead of man the key to sex. They recommend wholesale abandonment on the ground that all repression is bad. This theory forgets, however, that every expression involves repression of some kind. If I repress stealing, I express honesty; if I repress anger, I express compatibility.

F.D., 36

Reputation

Reputation is often only popularity, and, like a breeze, it cannot be kept.

D.L., 14

The most lasting reputations are those that are achieved after death when the tinsel of empty glory fades away. The greatness of Lincoln is posthumous. The glory of Christ came after His Crucifixion.

D.L., 15

Anyone who enjoys the world's repute, if he is honest with himself, knows that he does not deserve it.

D.L., 15

Resolutions

Resolutions, like the good, die young.

T.T., 170

Responsibility

Cabbages, horses, adding machines, boots, ships and sealing wax cannot sin, because they have no freedom, therefore no responsibility. To deny sin is therefore to reduce man to the status of a *thing*.

G.C., 17

Rest

Rest is the imperative of creation.

D.L., 47

What the Savior promises in the retirement is "rest for your souls." Rest is a gift—it is not earned; it is not the payment for finishing a job; it is the dowry of grace.

O.B., 62

Restitution

Restitution is a duty which a civilization which stresses profits and money can readily forget.

W.I., 41

The Resurrection

If there is no Resurrection, but Christ is dead, one cannot believe either in the Goodness of God or the goodness of man. But if He Who took the worst the world had to offer and conquered it, then evil shall never be victorious again.

E.I., 39

The Resurrection is the only answer to the question of the breach that we all feel psychologically in ourselves between the body and the soul. Some thinkers through the ages sacrificed the body to the soul; today the tendency is to sacrifice the soul to the body. The Resurrection reveals the sacredness of both.

W.I., 184

Retirement

The mind often grows stronger with age; hence the ridiculousness of enforced retirement at sixty-five.

O.B., 195

Silence helps speech; retirement helps thinking.

W.H., 139

Revelation and Faith

Revelation and faith, be it understood, do not mean doing violence to our reason. Faith no more destroys reason than a telescope destroys the vision.

R.G., 338

Revolution

All that economic and political revolutions do is to shift booty and loot from one party's pocket to another. For that reason, none of them is really revolutionary: they all leave greed in the heart of man.

L.A., 104

Revolution (Christian)

Revolution within the soul is the Christian adventure. It requires no hatred, demands no personal rights, claims no exalted titles, tells no lies. In such a revolution, it is love which bores from within and acts as a Fifth Column, loyal to God, within our tangled and disordered selves. . . . The sword it carries is not turned against our neighbor, but against our absurd over-valuation of the self. In other revolutions, it is easy to fight, for it is against the "evil enemy" that we are at war. But the Christian revolution is difficult, for the enemy we must assault is a part of us.

W.H., 40-41

Revolutionary Movement

The great fallacy of all revolutionary movements is that the value of great lives is nullified, either through persecution or character assassination, in the interests of fallacious promises and illusory hopes.

W.I., 68

Reward

The Lord in the end will reward us not on the basis of our activity, but on our faithfulness in His cause.

M.P., 253

Riches

Riches in great abundance have a peculiar quality; they make men more greedy.

D.L., 12

Ridicule

One of the penalties of being religious is to be mocked and ridiculed. If Our Lord submitted Himself to the ribald humour of a degenerate Tetrarch, we may be sure that we, His followers, will not escape. The more Divine a religion is, the more the world will ridicule you, for the spirit of the world is the enemy of Christ.

C.P., 56

Rights (Minority)

The one great truth which must not be surrendered is that basic minority rights, in the sense of human rights, endure regardless of the arithmetic of an election.

F.G., 163

Rocking Chair

The rocking chair, it has been said, is a typical American invention; it enables man to rest as he is restless, to sit in one place and still be on the go.

L.H., 140

Romantic Ideal

The Romantic ideal stressed feelings and emotions; it made an emotional or sentimental outlook on mankind the test of human goodness. Jean Jacques Rousseau, who fostered this ideal, once boasted: "I believe that there is not in the entire world a more humble man than I." Feeling good was made equivalent to being good, provided that one did not regard any one experience or moment in life as the totality of life itself.

D.L., 71

Romanticist

The romanticist influence on literature manifested itself in a protest against classicism, asserting that the only true unity was the unity of feeling. Its three dominating notes were: first, intuition as the means by which we ascend from clear consciousness to the absolute; secondly, an identification of nature and consciousness; thirdly, pantheism, or an ecstatic and mystic fusion of man and nature, divinity and humanity.

P.O., 45

The romanticist loves love.

T.M., 11

Rosary

The Rosary is the book of the blind, where souls see and there enact the greatest drama of love the world has ever known; it is the book of the simple, which initiates them into mysteries and knowledge more satisfying than the education of other men; it is the book of the aged, whose eyes close upon the shadow of this world, and open on the substance of the next. The power of the Rosary is beyond description.

W.L., 183

Rousseau, Jean-Jacques

If a man does not suit his life to an idea, he w   an idea and suit it to his life. If we do not live as we think,   oon begin to think as we live. So Jean Jacques, who glori   notion, now formed a philosophy to suit his sensuality—the   sophy of Romanticism, or the glorification of the sentiment   o.

L.5, 263

Royalty (American)

Despite the equality which democracy seeks, it nevertheless is in constant struggle to keep up with the Joneses. We boast that we have no royalty in America, and we disdain all that it implies, but what American has ever been invited to the Court of St. James who has not accepted? And though we frown upon kings and queens, we nevertheless, have our "copper kings," our "asparagus kings," our "cotton queens," and our "Sugar Bowl queens." But it is a good and healthy sign that we never outgrow our love of fairy stories, of humor, of heroes and of saints, and even of princesses.

L.5, 35

Russia

Russia is the home of godlessness, but Russia could just as well have the mission to Christianize modern Europe as to give it anti-Christ. Its history has been full of a Messianic consciousness that it was destined to give something to the world, and its present pains could just as well be the pangs of birth as the groan of death.

C.C., 209

A typical instance of this abandonment of morality based on God and His justice is the tendency in international relations to call Russia a "friendly nation" when the facts prove that Russia has been just as destructive of humanity, as hateful of religion, as oppressive of the masses and as cruel to hearts as the Nazis—and that is as damning an indictment as could be made of any nation.

G.C., 67

Russia (Communism in)

The basic reason why communism appealed to Russia was religious. Deeply imbedded in the Russian soul were passionate religious convictions: the universal vocation of Russia to call all men to brotherhood, the need of sacrifice and pain to accomplish this mission, and the supreme need of resigning oneself to God's will. Communism in the face of a declining Church promised the people the realization of these three ideals, but without clearly telling them that they would be emptied of God. Brotherhood became a revolutionary proletariat; sacrifice became violence, and the Will of God became the will of the dictator. Communism is a religion, a surrender to an absolute. That is why it appeals to those who are without faith, and why *Soviet Russia is today regarded as the last hope of the Western man who lives without God.*

C.C., 190

Russian Revolution

The Communist Revolution, at least in its beginnings, repudiated a thousand years of Christianity which was so deeply rooted in the Russian soul that the word for peasant and Christian *(krestianin)* were identical.

s.p., 18

S

Sacraments

The Sacraments are the drama of God.

P.R., 110

The humanity of Christ was the bearer of divine life and the means of making men holy; the sacraments were also to become the effective signs of the sanctification purchased by His death. As Our Blessed Lord was the sensible sign of God, so the sacraments were to become the sensible signs of the grace which Our Lord had won for us.

T.A., 10

Sacrifice

The law that runs through Nature is *there is never a sacrament without a sacrifice*. Nothing contributes to our living except through something that has experienced dying. Here is the fallacy of those who would reduce the Eucharist to a meal—What meat is ever put on a dish except through its death? It seems a hard law, but it is true; *we live by what we slay.* We slew Him by our sins. But through His Mercy we live by what we have slain. There is a Communion because there has been a Consecration; there is a oneness with the Holiness of His Priesthood because there is a Cross in our Victimhood.

M.P., 160

Love is the soul of sacrifice.

M.U., 55

How many people there are in Church on Sunday sitting in the first seat of the pew, who resent anyone asking them to "please move over." They came to kneel before a cross, but they do not want one standing alongside them.

W.I., 91

Sacrifice and Love

The day men forget that love is synonymous with sacrifice, that day they will ask what selfish sort of woman it must have been who ruthlessly extracted tribute in the form of flowers, or what an avaricious creature she must have been who demanded solid gold in the form of a ring, just as they will ask what cruel kind of God is it who asks for sacrifice and self-denial.

L.L., 95

Saint

. . . saints who measure themselves by the Infinite, are absolutely convinced of their nothingness. Thomas Aquinas said all that he had written was a straw when he was bequeathed a vision of the truth of God.

L.4, 210

Ask a man: "Are you a saint?" If he answers in the affirmative, you can be very sure that he is not.

W.H., 18

"Saint" (Communist)

The Communist "saints" preach bastard brotherhood without the fatherhood of God, and sacrifice themselves on picket lines for the sake of economic ideals. They have secularized the Beatitudes; at every step they say that the low shall become the high; the last shall be first; the overlooked shall be the preferred; the poor shall be rich; the scorned shall be reverenced; that old truth shall be the error, and man shall be reborn. They have perverted truth and the Gospel; they have turned the announcement into their reannouncement; they have taken the Pentecostal fires and made them burn downward instead of upward; they have made *this world* all-important.

M.W., 192–193

St. Francis of Assisi

If St. Francis had been sent to a Siberian labor camp, or to a leper colony, or to a Wall Street brokerage firm, would he be any less a St. Francis? But how many mortals there are in the world who are one kind of character in need, another kind of character in plenty, who grumble amidst the uncomfortable, and who become possessed by possessions. St. Francis remains the same in all circumstances; the non-St. Francis types, like a chameleon, take on the color of the leaf on which they rest.

G.T., 144

Sainthood

The essence of sanctity is the external love of mankind as sons of God, because of the interior love of the Father—*it does not take much time to make us saints—it takes only much love.*

F.D., 256

Saintliness

Every theologian ought to be a mystic; every D.D., or Doctor of Divinity, ought to be a saint. He *knows* enough to be one; but he does not *will* it, or work hard enough at it.

L.I, 76

Salvation

The greatest inspiration in the moral order is the Life of our Blessed Lord and particularly His death on the Cross. By it He emphasized that the salvation of a soul is worth more than the gaining of the whole world. Salvation is based on the paradox that he who loses his life for time shall save it for eternity.

M.U., 150

Salvation must come from without because you can destroy life, but you cannot create it; you can blind your vision but you cannot restore it; you can destroy your communion with God by sin, but you cannot restore it.

P.R., 57

Sanctity

There is nothing so base or low that it cannot be reconquered; there is no duty, however menial, that cannot be retrieved for sanctity; and that there is nothing that is cast down that cannot be lifted up.

M.P., 235

Satan

Do not mock the Gospels and say there is no Satan. Evil is too real in the world to say that. Do not say the idea of Satan is dead and gone. Satan never gains so many cohorts, as when, in his shrewdness, he spreads the rumor that he is long since dead. Do not reject the Gospel because it says the Saviour was tempted. Satan always tempts the pure—the others are already his. Satan stations more devils on monastery walls than in dens of iniquity, for the latter offer no resistance. Do not say it was absurd that Satan should appear to Our Lord, for Satan must always come close to the godly and the strong—the others succumb from a distance.

E.G., 56–57

Satan possesses only willing victims.

P.N., 223

Scandal

If there were scandals associated with His Physical Life, so that He prayed that His followers would not be scandalized in Him, why should we not expect scandals in His Body, the Church? When we see a few leaving the Church today, does this prove that she is not

His Body, any more than He was not Divine when "they all left Him and fled"?

Scholar as Skeptic

Such a man projects his own mental confusion to the outside world and concludes that, since he knows no truth, nobody can know it.

P.S., 7

Science

Science cannot give us a philosophy, nor can it give us an ethics; it cannot give us a philosophy, because it immerses man in nature and avoids the important subject of his destiny. It cannot give us an ethics because science by itself is amoral. Morality comes from its ends, and science is indifferent to ends.

P.O., 117

The rock-sureness of "Science" does not exist in the mind of the scientists themselves, though it does live and throb in the minds of publicists and propagandists. Scientists themselves disclaim they possess ultimate truth; rather they look upon it as a horizon toward which they are proceeding.

R.G., 231

Science and Theology

There is humility and there is prudence in the caution of scientists when they speak of their theories as hypotheses, but there is no humility and no prudence in the recklessness with which philosophers of religion apply these hypotheses to religion. Religion is not to be made the proving ground of every scientific hypothesis any more than the soul is to be made the puppet of every demand of the body.

R.G., 245

Science and Tolerance

Disagreeing with science is considered as vicious as disagreeing with the multiplication table, but to disagree about religious fundamentals is like disagreeing with the World Court.

R.G., 250

Science versus History

Science is a record of what is happening, whereas history is a record of what *matters*.

O.B., 230

Scientific Theory

What is the essential difference between the old Greek theory that the world was made of four elements—air, earth, fire, and water—and the modern scientific theory that it is made up of electrical energy diversified into ninety-two elements? Really, the only difference is a difference in the exactness of measurement, not a difference in interpretation of the whole. . . . The old Greeks measured crudely in yards; we measure skilfully in millimeters. They called things "chunks of matter," we call them "electrical charges." This certainly is an advance in the delicacy of measurement, but it is not necessarily an advance in the final explanation of things in terms of the First Cause, Which is God.

O.E., 156-157

Scientism

Science says "this," or science says "that," is the last word to be said on any subject. Hence there is no place for values, tradition, metaphysics, revelation, faith, authority, or theology. God has no purposes in the universe; first of all because there is no God, and secondly because there are no purposes. Scientism does not say we ignore purposes in our laboratory, but rather we eliminate purposes from the universe.

P.W., 51

When Comte developed sociology, then everything was socialized, even God; when Darwin developed evolution, then everything was evolutionized, including morals; now that relativity has been established, non-scientists make everything relative, saying there is no such thing as Truth or Goodness—these are relative to your point of view. Quite apart from the fact that the theory of relativity does not deny an absolute—for it is based on the absoluteness of the spread of light—it is rather absurd to apply the methods of one branch of knowledge to all other branches of knowledge.

W.I., 22

Scientist

The scientist does not tell nature its laws; nature tells the scientist.

W.I., 148

Seat Belts

There is something psychologically profound in the present custom of putting safety belts in new automobiles to offer safety in times of wreck. Our melancholic age is looking forward to disaster even when on a pleasure trip.

L.4, 51

Secularism

Secularism means the separation of the parts of life,—for example, education, politics and economics and family,—from their center, which is God. Each department of life is considered as having absolute autonomy and in no way can be brought under the sway of ethical principles or the sovereign Law of God. Secularism reaches its peak when men say, "business is business," and "religion is religion," as if the way a man worked or the pay he gave to workers had nothing to do with conscience and the moral fibre of a nation.

P.W., 35

Seminaries

In the days immediately following Vatican Council II, seminaries rightly began training the seminarians in social and pastoral activities, but wrongly neglected discipline and the spiritual life. The result was that no sooner were the young chicks hatched than they ran with foxes.

M.P., 132

Serenity

Only the man who is self-possessed is serene, for he alone has set up conditions for peace which are under his own control.

W.H., 125

Servant

. . . no man has a right to command until he has learned to serve, and no man has a right to be a master until he has learned to be a servant, and no man has a right to power until he has learned to be obedient.

E.G., 42

Service

True Christian greatness is measured not by superiority, but by service: "And he that will be first among you, shall be your servant." (Matthew 20:27) The greatest race on earth is the race that renders the most service to others in the name of God.

L.A., 159

The vertical relationship to God has, to some extent, been abandoned in favor of a horizontal relationship to man. Service is taking the place of prayer. The Mount of the Transfiguration is abandoned for the sake of the sick boy and the distraught father in the valley below. Marys are leaving the feet of Christ to become Marthas of the Inner City. The sacred is identified with the secular; the Kingdom of God becomes the Kingdom of Man.

M.P., 16

Self

It is all very well and good to release men from certain anxieties, but the real cure does not come until one is released *to* a concern for the welfare of others. The cruelest words of tongue or pen are, "I could not have cared less." The ungiven self is an unfulfilled self.

F.D., 106

Self-complacency

The moment we become self-complacent about our achievements, the work spoils in our hands.

P.N., 125

Self-denial

The purpose of asceticism, self-denial and mortification is the growth in charity or love of God. Christian self-denial is not based on the idea that the world, or the flesh are intrinsically wicked, but on the conviction that God is intrinsically good.

D.L., 65

Self-discipline

The modern world is opposed to self-discipline on the ground that personality must be "self-expressive."

L.A., 93

Self-examination

Self-examination must be done in the presence of God—we must compare ourselves *not* with our *neighbor,* nor with our own subjective ideals, but with the Perfect.

L.A., 80

Selfishness

Selfishness is the world's greatest sin; that is why the world hates those who hate it, why it is jealous of those who have more; why it is envious of those who do more; why it dislikes those who refuse to flatter.

C.B., 6

The sign of the end of the world will be selfishness.

L.A., 114

Self-knowledge

Self-knowledge is not intellectual, but moral. It falls not within the domain of psychology, but theology; it is concerned not with what we think, but with our motives and the hidden springs of life and action.

L.A., 80

Self-reflection

About the only time some people do any reflecting is when they look in a mirror, and that's the wrong kind of reflection.

L.4, 9

Self-restraint

If there is any one lesson which our modern civilization finds it difficult to learn, it is the necessity of self-restraint.

D.L., 108

Self-worship

If you do not worship God, you worship something, and nine times out of ten it will be yourself. If there is no God, then you are a god; and if you are a god and your own law and your own creator, then we ought never to be surprised that there are so many atheists.

P.R., 17

Sex

Sex divorced from love, instead of raising man by taking him away from himself, drags him down to the hall of mirrors where he is always confronted with self. Sex does not care about the person, but about the act. The fig leaf which once was put over the secret parts of man and woman in sculpture is now put over the face. The person does not matter.

M.P., 314

The Victorians pretended it did not exist; the moderns pretend that nothing else exists.

P.S., 137

It is not just a physiological experience, but the unraveling of a mystery.

T.M., 125

Sex Education

It is . . . argued that if young people knew the evil effects of the excesses of sex, and were told of their consequences, they would have no urge to abuse sex, just as they would have no urge to go into a house where there was a smallpox quarantine sign. The argument is fallacious, first of all, because such a position fosters only hygiene and not character; secondly, it does not make allowances for every individual's believing that he will escape the evil effects. More important still, it forgets that no young person has an urge to break down a door on which a quarantine sign is written, but everyone has a sex urge, which needs considerable control.

G.T., 57

The fallacy of sex education is assuming that if children know the evil effects of certain acts, they will abstain from those acts.

S.W., 19

The Sexes

. . . man governs the home, but the woman reigns in it.

O.B., 254

Sheen, Fulton J.

How God will judge I know not, but I trust that He will see me with mercy and compassion. I am only certain that there will be three surprises in Heaven. First of all, I will see some people there whom I never expected to see. Second, there will be a number whom I expect to be there who will not be there. And, even relying on His mercy, the biggest surprise of all may be that I will be there.

A., 6

It is said that I am an orator, and in weak moments I believe it—but only for the reason that when I finish speaking I notice there is always a great "awakening."

L.2, 59

Normally, priests are ordained at the age of twenty-four. I was ordained at twenty-four, but evidently must have been mentally retarded for I was sent to universities for five more years.

L.2, 213

Sickness

There is nothing that so much adds to the longevity of sickness as a long face.

W.H., 24

Silence

Silence is not a privation of stillness, nor a muteness, nor an emptiness; it is a communion by which one attains truths above creation and action.

L.4, 140

Action is the great need of the Eastern World; silence the need of the Western. The East with its fatalism does not believe that man does anything; the West with its actionism believes that man does everything. Somewhere in between is the golden mean wherein silence prepares for action. He who holds his tongue for a day will speak much more wisely tomorrow.

W.I., 147–148

Sin

Sin is the abandonment of God by man; it is the creature forsaking the Creator, as a flower might abandon the sunlight which gave its strength and beauty. Sin is a separation, a divorce—the original divorce from unity with God, whence all other divorces are derived.

C.M., 60

Sin is the abuse of freedom; that is why the modern man, who denied sin, found himself in a world of dictatorship.

G.W., 38

If you choose to offend God, successful you may be, honored you may be, rich you may be, praised by the world you may be, "broadminded" and "progressive" you may be, alive to public opinion and to the new morals of the day you may be, but you will never know how much you have failed, as Barabbas never knew how much he failed the day of his success. But you will be dead! dead to the life of Christ! dead to the love of God! dead to the ageless peacefulness of eternity!

H.C., 25

The gravest danger facing modern society, one which has brought the ruin of older civilizations and is destined to effect the collapse of our own unless we prevent it is the loss of the sense of sin. . . . There is a general denial that anything is wrong or that anything is right, and a general affirmation that what the older theological generation called "sin" is only a psychic evil or a fall in the evolutionary process.

H.C., 72

Nature tells us that sin is death; conscience tells us that sin is guilt; and God tells us that sin is an offence against His Divine Love.

H.C., 73

What death is to the body, that sin is to the soul.

L.A., 73

Sin is in the blood. Every doctor knows this; even passers-by can see it. Drunkenness is in the eyes, the bloated cheek. Avarice is written in the hands and on the mouth. Lust is written in the eyes. There is not a libertine, a criminal, a bigot, a pervert who does not have his hate or his envy written in every inch of his body, every hidden gateway and alley of his blood, and every cell of his brain.

L.C., 322

Poverty is serious; the inner-city is a reproach; cartels are a blotch on a nation's justice; war is the pus from the inner corruption of egotism—but there is also guilt, sin, adultery, fornication, greed, hypocrisy which comes from inside the heart and spoils the world.

M.P., 174

The last and crowning act of sin is the rejection of Him Who made us conscious of sin. Without Him we could sin in peace. With Him, we see sin as the nailing of Goodness to a tree. The individual conscience will be seared and burned by the Spirit to recognize that it is not Grade B milk or insufficient playgrounds which cause our ruin, but our own sin.

M.P., 282

No one has ever come to the twenties—let alone the forties, the fifties, the sixties or the seventies of life—without reflecting on himself and the world round about him, and without knowing the tension that sin causes in the soul. Faults and follies do not efface themselves from the record of memory; sleeping tablets do not silence them; psychoanalysts cannot explain them away. While the sun of youth shines bright, it may blind the eye momentarily so that the outline of sin is obscure. But then comes a time of clarity —a sick bed, a sleepless night, the open sea, a moment of quiet, the innocence in the face of a child—when our sins, like spectres or phantoms, burn their unrelenting characters of fire upon our consciences. Their full seriousness may not have been realized in the moment of passion, but conscience bides its time. It will bear its stern uncompromising witness sometime, somewhere. It will force a dread upon the soul, a dread designed to make it cast itself back again to God. Such a soul experiences indescribable agonies and tortures, yet they are only a drop of the entire ocean of humanity's guilt which overwhelmed the Savior as if they were His own in the Garden.

P.N., 169

A man sins, not because he is ignorant, but because he is perverse. The intellect makes mistakes, but the will sins.

P.W., 74

All sin is self-mutilation.

S.V., 93

He who is conscious of sin looks into his own breast to find the culprit, but he who denies guilt must always look to his neighbor.

T.T., 82

Sin, in all its forms, is the deliberate eviction of Love from the soul. Sin is the enforced absence of Divinity.

W.L., 194

Sin and the Sinner

. . . love and hate can cease to be incompatible if their objects are different: e.g., I can love the Communist, feed his hungry children, pay his rent, give him my seat in a subway. But I hate Communism; it is intrinsically wicked. In other words, love the sinner, hate his sin.

D.D., 66

Sin (Denial of)

Sin is not the worst thing in the world; the worst thing is the denial of sin. If I am blind and deny light, I shall never see; if I am deaf and deny sound, I shall never hear. If I am a sinner and deny sin, there is no forgiveness. The denial of sin is the unforgivable sin.

M.P., 281

The Sincere

The sincere are those who have an ensemble of virtues, who are equally good at speaking and listening; who have silences, as well as words; who are not opaque like curtains, but transparent like window panes. They speak, knowing that one day they will have to be judged by God.

W.I., 85

Singing

To sing a song is to possess one's soul. Maria, the sister of Moses, sang after the miraculous crossing of the Red Sea. Deborah sang after the defeat of the Canaanites. Wherever liberty is, there the free sing.

W.L., 34

Sinless

That Figure on the Cross bore to the full not only the physical effects of sin which any man might suffer, and not only the mental effects of sin which all of us ought to feel, but the spiritual effects of sin which only He could feel because being sinless He was not part of it. Only the sinless know the horror of sin.

S.V., 84

Skeptic

The old sceptic denied that reason could know anything above the sensible world; the new sceptic denies he can know anything except what is below the sensible world, namely, in the unconscious.

W.I., 137

Slavery

The old slavery was only physical. The slave owner did not care how the slave used his soul, or even if he had a soul. He was concerned only with his labor. The new slavery, however, takes hold not only of the body of a man, but also of his soul. It lays hold of the more divine part of him and asserts that he shall not call his property his own, or even his soul his own. He belongs to the State as its draft horse, forced to enrich it as the Communists say the Capitalists forced the proletarians to enrich them.

C., 88

Our Blessed Lord said nothing about slavery, because He knew that slavery would never be eradicated until men saw themselves related to one another on the basis of equality as children of God.

S.C., 48

Slavery (Invited)

There are three ways in which a man becomes a slave. He may be born into slavery, or forced into it, or he can deliberately accept his servitude. All three forms flourish in the modern world. Men are born and forced into slavery in Russia and her satellite states. Men in the free world invite slavery when they ask the government to provide complete security, when they surrender their freedom to the "welfare state."

O.B., 138

Slob (Age of the)

As the Soviets have substituted a bourgeois style of life for the "working class elite," so today some disciples of Christ have abandoned the Christ-life to be more suited to their secular environment. It is not the Christ-model that determines their lives; it is the mentality of their group. As some clergy compromised with the ruling monarchy of Louis XIV, and later compromised with the capitalism of the nineteenth century, so today some are compromising with the mass-secularism of the twentieth century as *the Age of the Snob gives way to the Age of the Slob.*

M.P., 132

Sloth

Sloth is a malady of the will which causes neglect of one's duty. In the physical realm it appears as laziness, softness, idleness, procrastination, nonchalance, and indifference; as a spiritual disease, it takes the forms of a distaste of the spiritual, lukewarmness at prayers, and contempt of self-discipline. Sloth is the sin of those who only look at picture-magazines, but never at print; who read only novels, but never a philosophy of life. Sloth disguises itself as tolerance and broad-mindedness—it has not enough intellectual energy to discover Truth and follow it. Sloth loves nothing, hates nothing, hopes nothing, fears nothing, keeps alive because it sees nothing to die for. It rusts out rather than wears out; it would not render a service to any employer a minute after a whistle blows; and the more it increases in our midst, the more burdens it throws upon the State. Sloth is ego-centrical; it is basically an attempt to escape from social and spiritual responsibilities, in the expectation that someone else will care for us. The lazy man is a parasite. He demands that others cater to him and earn his bread for him; he is asking special privileges in wishing to eat bread which he has not earned.

L.H., 71

Sloth is a malady of the will which causes us to neglect our duties. Sloth may be either physical or spiritual. It is physical when it manifests itself in laziness, procrastination, idleness, softness, indifference, and nonchalance. It is spiritual when it shows itself in an indifference to character betterment, a distaste for the spiritual, a hurried crowding of devotions, a lukewarmness and failure to cultivate new virtue.

V.V., 73

Sloth (Mental)

Mental laziness also confuses the "latest" with the "important." A disdain for tradition, a contempt for history which makes the past irrelevant is like losing one's memory; the present and the future are without the wisdom of the past. Mental laziness, above all, manifests itself in skepticism or the certitude that nothing is certain. The uncommitted mind is lazy because it never closes on anything.

L.4, 58

Smile

A smile is laughter's whisper and has its roots in the soul.

L.2, 32

Snob

Snobbery sneers at the higher position of others, because the snobs want to sit in their chairs and enjoy their applause. They assume that in not arriving at such popular favor themselves they were deprived of their due. That is why we hate those who do not pay sufficient attention to us and why we love those who flatter us.

V.V., 16

Social Engineer

The post-war planners are still assuming with Marx that man is essentially economic, or with Darwin that he is essentially animal, or with Freud that he is essentially sexual, or with Hitler that he is essentially political. Hence they think that all we have to do is to change an economic system, or form new parties, or give more sex instruction, or greater license to the break-up of the family and we will have peace.

P.W., 95

Social Engineering

A planned society is a slave society.

O.B., 261

Social Justice

. . . what forces are best suited to give to our government this very desirable stability? Will the forces of birth-control which limit the number of our citizens by refusing to bring into the world the very units of democratic social life make for its stability? Will the loose divorce laws of our country, which break up families, the very core of national life, make for its endurance? Will the loose morality, which believes that anything is right providing one is not caught, make for a strong and disciplined and stable nation? These are the forces which are decaying and breaking down our national life. But the only single force in America to-day which opposes these destructive elements is the spiritual force of the Church.

M.T., 183

Social Reform

Modern social reform begins with the group and ends with the group. Modern morality talks about crime, which is a group problem; the Church in the confessional talks to the criminal, which is the individual problem.

M.T., 54

Social Service

The proper balance is found . . . in the story of Martha and Mary which follows in the Gospel the Good Samaritan. In the latter, social service is praised. But in the story of Martha and Mary, it is suggested that we are not to become too absorbed in serving, that we have no time to sit at the feet of Jesus and learn His lessons.

M.P., 20

Identification with others is the condition of true social service.

M.P., 67

Social Work

If God appears dead in our nuclear age, it is because Christians and arid people have isolated Christ from His Cross. Some priests and religions have love enough for the hungry, but not love enough to redeem from guilt. The priest, in order to relate himself better to the world, may preach a "social Christ" or a "political Christ" or a "revolutionary Christ," but such indifference to the crucifixion produce sermons that are "sounding brass and clinking cymbals." The intellectual and moral commitment of the priest to the Sermon on the Mount needs also the existential surrender to the prolongation of the Cross. Mother Teresa of Calcutta expressed this idea: "Serving of the poor without the love of Christ crucified is social work."

M.P., 33

Socialism

. . . as men become indifferent to right and wrong, disorder and chaos increase, and the State steps in to organize the chaos by force. Dictatorships arise in such a fashion. Such is the essence of Socialism, the compulsory organization of chaos.

P.R., 193

Socialism is no answer . . . simply because Socialism is not social. Any State which concentrates property in its hands is the enemy of the people.

S.P., 56

Society (Modern)

Modern society is what might be characterized as acquisitive, for its primary concern is to acquire, to own, to possess; its aristocracy is not one of blood or virtue, but of money; it judges worth not by righteousness but in terms of possessions.

C.B., 53

Socrates

How the modern world needs a Socrates, who used to walk into the market place of Athens asking people questions in order to make them discover themselves! True, he was put to death for unmasking others, but he left the world the heritage of "know thyself."

G.T., 80

Solitude

. . . most people have a dread of being alone, without knowing why the prospect frightens them.

W.H., 26

Only in solitariness is true spirituality born, when the soul stands naked before its God.

W.I., 149

Soul

. . . all the beauties of nature do not compare in the smallest degree with the beauty of a soul in the state of grace . . . [the Christian knows] that the soul of a Bowery derelict is more precious in the sight of God than the success of any world policy; that it really does not matter very much whether children ever confuse Aristides with Aristotle, but it does matter if they confuse Buddha with Christ; . . . that poverty is not the greatest curse; that physical infirmity is not the greatest ill; that the loss of a member of a family is not so serious as the loss of faith. . . .

M.T., 131

Unless souls are saved, nothing is saved.

P.S., 3

The passing of time wears out bodies, but nothing can make a soul vanish or can diminish its eternal value. Nothing.

T.M., 186

Soul versus State

If the soul belongs to the State, then it is treason to the State, to dare offer it to God. This is the reason why the Catholic Church is termed "counter-revolutionary" in Mexico and in Russia and Spain. An atheistic State knows full well that it cannot completely possess man as the tool of the State, unless it unmakes the Church which says that man is also a child of God; and that it cannot enslave man until it enslaves the Church which says that man is free.

C.C., 84

Soviet Constitution

. . . the Soviet Constitution sets up the dictatorship of the proletariat in one hundred and seventeen articles before it mentions a single right, and then, under Article 125, conditions all rights upon the furtherance of Communism.

W.W., 73

Soviet Union

It talks peace but prepares for war; it forbids strikes in Russia but incites them here; it rightly protests against violence directed towards it, and yet insists on the right to use violence on others; it builds a Paradise by first making a wreck of the world; it establishes a classless class by throwing classes at one another's throats; it boasts that it does away with two classes, and yet establishes in its own country about nineteen classes of privilege; it urges all labor unions to a general strike, but yet purges all who would think of it in their fatherland.

L.E., 53

It reduces man to an animal by regarding him as an ant whose business it is to pile up more wealth for the State; it deprives his moral actions of a natural basis by declaring he has no other destiny than that of a faithful horse in a collectivist farm. It then upsets that belief by mummifying Lenin, for if the destiny of both Lenin and a horse is the same, why glorify one more than another?

. L.E., 152

Speaking

Think before you speak; then talk to yourself.

D.L., 134

The whirlwind on the tongue is the sign of the tempest in the soul.

D.L., 135

Speech

Speech is the summation of a soul: all that it has been, all that it is, and all that it will ever be.

L.2, 4

Speech (Freedom of)

Is there a limit to tolerance, say, of freedom of speech? Yes, there is a limit to freedom of speech. It is reached when we use freedom of speech to destroy freedom of speech. Anyone in the world may use freedom of speech, as long as he allows anyone else to enjoy that freedom of speech. But there are those who would use this freedom of speech to deny that right to others. Toward that latter group we ought to be intolerant. That is why the Communists differ from any other group in a democracy. Even those people who are called "crackpots" are willing to let anyone else be a "crackpot." But Communists will not allow anyone to be a non-Communist.

L.1, 163

Spengler's *Decline of the West*

Is it any wonder that thoughtful men are beginning to write and speak of the Decline of the West? Spengler, Massis, and a host of others, in making a retrospect of our Western World, are right in saying that it is on the decline. Many of them are wrong only in their explanation. It is not machinery, nor finance, nor naval armaments, nor the amassing of gold, nor rigorous iron laws of determinism, which have effected this decline. The two decisive factors

in the breakdown of Western Civilization have been the two causes
. . . —mass-defection from Christ and mass-defection from God.

P., 15

The Spiritual

The primacy of the spiritual means that there is nothing in the world that really matters except the salvation of our soul, and that in its salvation the spiritual must reign over the temporal, the soul over the body, grace over nature, and God over the world. Religion means this or it means nothing.

M.T., 125–126

Spiritual Life

Nothing so much cripples the spiritual life as these hidden "bugs" in the motor of our soul, such as self-seeking, immorality, dishonesty and bitterness toward others. We wonder why, when we seem to advance so far, that we suffer such defeats. Invariably it is because of the "Fifth Column" of prejudices and evil habits and the Trojan horse of dominant fault. Until that is dug out and laid before God, there can be no real progress in the spirit.

D.L., 62

Spirituality

The Cain tradition of spirituality makes no mention of guilt, sin or atonement. If Christ is mentioned, He is "used" to support a position already taken: "Jesus and Revolution," "Jesus and Militancy," "Jesus and Homosexuality," "Jesus and the Secular City."

M.P., 106

Standard

Society can live only by standards of right and wrong.

W.I., 131

The State

Forget the ultimate destiny of man and a new god will be created for him—a cruel god which is the tyrannical State. When Rome forgot its religion it deified its emperors; when Western Civilization forgets its Christianity, it begins to deify the State.

C.C., 70–71

The State (Absolute)

State absolutism has become such a nurse of the people that it has not only taken over their property, it has even taken over their souls. It possesses man from the cradle to the grave, by denying that he has any end and purpose other than the service of the State. Hence the elimination of the unfit, sterilization, birth-control clinics . . . hence the tendency of the State to take over the functions of religion, and substitute a worship of the State for the worship of God, as is done in Russia, in Mexico, and to some extent in Germany; hence the movement to allow psychology to take the place of theology, psychoanalysis to take the place of a confessor, cures to take the place of penance, teachers to take the place of the clergy, and clinics to take the place of the Church. . . . Thus it is that man who was once free to do anything, is now free to do nothing; man who once was so individual that he could worship any God he wished is now mechanized and depersonalized until he has no more individuality than a pea in a pod.

C.C., 174–175

The State (Modern)

It is illuminating to observe that in every State in the modern world where there has been universal conscription *to the exclusion of God,* there has been erected a slave state.

D.D., 129

The State (Socialist)

There are four steps upwards to the modern socialistic State. The first was the false principle of the sixteenth century that the religion of the State was the religion of its prince, by which national churches were substituted for a Catholic or universal Church. The second step was the Age of Reason in which the State became secularized by divorcing politics from ethics, and economics from morality. The third step was Marxian Socialism in which the Church was liquidated by the State. And the fourth step is Nazism where the State is substituted for the Church.

P.W., 114

Statistics

Statistics appear now and then that the majority of Catholic women are practicing abortion; whether it is true or not, the fact remains that many do. The assumption created by such statistics, by gathering names of priests or nuns against a moral truth of the Church is that the sheer force of numbers prove that they are right. Both at Kadesh and in our times, it can be crucifying to trust in the Church and its Pontiff. But God did not give up His people then, any more than now. Intercession must be made by those who are not "with it" for those who are "with it." "Forgive their iniquity, I beseech Thee," cried Moses "as befits thy great and constant love" (Numbers 14:19).

M.P., 142

Status Quo

A good simple soul on being asked the meaning of *status quo,* defined it rather correctly as the "mess we are in."

P.W., 167

Student (Modern)

Students are told that it is not so important to know anything; it is only important to know where to find it.

W.I., 124–125

Success

No true success is ever enjoyed without sacrifice and effort. If he who enjoys success did not pay for it, someone else did.

D.L., 68

The Successful

The tragedy of our day is the despair of the successful: their misery does not originate in the failure of their plans, but in the fact that, having realized them, they found no happiness. The Everything they longed to have (material benefits and temporal triumphs) turned out, on possession, to be Nothing.

W.H., 37

Suffering

Many persons identify themselves with their environment. Because life is good to them, they believe they are good. They never dwell on eternity because time is so pleasant. When suffering strikes, they become divorced from their pleasant surroundings and are left naked in their own souls. They then see that they were not really affable and genial, but irritable and impatient. When the sun of outer prosperity sank, they had no inner light to guide their darkened souls. It is, therefore, not what happens to us that matters; it is how we react to it.

L.A., 51

Some will not look on suffering because it creates responsibility.

M.P., 66

Suicide

The great numerical increase in suicide, which merits to be called suicidism, is symptomatic of a spiritual disintegration, a sapping of the will to live, a plunge into the irrational and the meaningless self-destruction.

P.R., 200–201

The Supernatural

The very heart of Christianity is the inspiration for man to strive to become something that he is not.

P.S., 238

Sympathy

Sympathy is a temper or character which draws others together. It is what might be called conductivity. The Greek origin of the word "sympathy" implies "suffering with." It is a kind of silent understanding when heart meets heart. It is a kind of substitution, in which one takes the heart out of his own body and places it in the body of another man, and in exchange takes back the other's heart.

F.D., 108

T

Talk

The great characteristic of our age is not its love of religion, but its love of talking about religion. Even those who would smite God from the heavens make a religion out of this irreligion, and a faith out of their doubt. On all sides—from a thousand pens, a hundred microphones, scores of university rostrums—we have heard it repeated, until our very head reels, that the "acids of modernity" have eaten away the old faith and the old morality, and that the modern man must have a new religion to suit the new spirit of the age.

E.G., 53

Ours is the most talkative age in history, not only because we can multiply words a million fold through radio and print, but also because there are few who like to be listeners.

W.I., 128

Teacher

I have found, after thirty years in universities, that the more books a professor brings into class, the less prepared he is. One of the greatest failures I ever knew as a teacher was one who used a cart to haul into the classroom his undigested but seeming knowledge.

G.T., 90

The teacher's work is no more finished just because he has a number of notes on his desk than the doctor's is just because he has a number of pills in his hand. Unless the patient assimilates the medicine, there is no cure, and unless the student assimilates the truth, there is no education.

L.5, 267

Teacher (Bad)

A football coach who does not produce a winning team is forced to leave. Old generals may fade away—but poor teachers are just handed on. Teaching often becomes a communication from the notebook of the teacher to the notebook of the student without passing through the minds of either.

A., 54

Teachers of Modern Morality

. . . the teachers of modern morality, advances beneath the same Cross, and who is there living in this great era of carnality who has not heard their taunts a thousand times as they sneer at the Church: "Come down from your belief in the sanctity of marriage! Come down from your belief in virginity and celibacy! Come down from your age-long opposition to divorce. Come down from your opposition to sex, when all the world is mad about it! Come down from your opposition to birth-control! Can you not see that the acids of modernity have eaten away your age-old morality. . . . It is easy to come down and follow the world, but it is nobler to remain suspended and draw the world to oneself. It is human to come down, but it is divine to hang there.

M.T., 214–215

Technology (Modern)

It is one of the curious anomalies of present day civilization that when man achieves greatest control over nature, he has the least control over himself. The great boast of our age is our domination of the universe: we have harnessed the waterfalls, made the wind a slave to carry us on wings of steel, and squeezed from the earth the secret of its age. Yet, despite this mastery of nature, there perhaps never was a time when man was less a master of himself. He is equipped like a veritable giant to control the forces of nature, but is as weak as a pigmy to control the forces of his passions and inclinations.

H.C., 34

Teenagers

As a youth loves speeding not in order to arrive some place, but just for the excitement of speeding, so too a teenager is apt to turn to the carnal to make up for the loss of purpose of life and society and family, by the intensity of an erotic experience. He seeks to destroy the mores which he knows to be corrupt, and to drag everyone down to his own level. Abandonment becomes a substitute for creativeness. He hopes to recover some compensation for what his sick soul has lost. Finding no home for the soul in the world, he becomes self-abandoned.

G.T., 33

Television

It is a fact that more crimes are committed in one year on television than in six major cities of the United States; a threat or an act of violence was enacted every two and one half minutes on children's television shows.

W.I., 102–103

Temperance

Temperance does not mean not drinking, not eating or not enjoying God-given instincts. It is rather the controlling of these excellencies in order that they may not run into faults. Some edible plants, for example, if they are allowed to go to seed, can poison a man; so a man's good qualities need to be kept under order, so that they be not exaggerated into weakness. As long as a man is master of his affections and desires, he can live in peace.

G.T., 55

Temptation

Not everybody is tempted in the same way: some are tempted to pervert the good instinct of self-preservation into egotism and selfishness; others, to pervert the good instinct of self-perpetuation through sex into lust; others are tempted to pervert the good instinct of self-extension through private property into avarice. And if one is tempted in any one of these three ways or in the way of intemperance, anger, envy, jealousy, gluttony, it is not because he is diseased: it is because, since the fall, goodness does not "come naturally," but with difficulty, and is overcome thoroughly only thanks to the supernatural.

P.S., 44

The best man to convert a drunkard is a converted drunkard. Power to appreciate temptation is the fine condition of being able to help others out of temptation.

W.I., 37

Thanks

Giving thanks is not weakness but strength, for it involves self-repression.

M.P., 223

Theater of the Absurd

The anti-spirit in art walks the stage in the Theater of the Absurd, in the plays of Ionesco, Jean Genet and Adamov; it slouches on campuses in those who hold that it is the business of society to support the universities until the students know enough to overthrow society. It genuflects in the sanctuary with anti-liturgy balloons, contrived prefaces and bare feet; in literature, the anti-hero acts out his emotions of cruelty, despair and remorse because he has lost his way and in the Church, by contempt of the Pope, and the damnation of the Church as an "institution." These anti-moods are like mountains on which humanity clings to "cliffs of fall." Security seems to be a dream, and disaster a certitude to those who know this anti-mood.

M.P., 134

Theism

A new crime is arising in the world today; be prepared for it. The crime of being a Christian. The crime of believing in God.

S.P., 112

Theologians (Liberal)

They never want to know whether a thing is right or wrong, but whether it is "progressive" or "reactionary," "liberal" or "contemporary"; they love to make distinctions between the "historical Jesus" and the "Christ of Paul" and say they would be Christian tomorrow if "all the accretions and perversions" were eliminated. They follow that one avocation in life in which there is no apprenticeship—criticism.

S.C., 85

Theology

In theology everything possesses its own objective value; it is true in itself, apart from our appreciation of it. Its dogmas are not barriers to thought. They are no more confining for a mind than plan, contour, and choice of colors are confining for an artist.

O.E., 126

Theology (Modern)

People are turning away from Christianity today not because it is too hard, but because it is too soft; not because it demands too much, but because it demands too little.

D.L., 180

. . . there is an increasing insistence on a new idea of God to suit democracy as a form of government. The War gave us the shibboleth, "Make the world safe for democracy": the philosopher echoed, "Make God safe for democracy."

G.I., 44

At the present time God is *really* denied; but *nominally* asserted. The next step will be to eliminate even the name.

R.G., 223

Thievery (Soviet)

Russia seized Finland and then justified its action on the ground that other nations might have invaded it. If that irrationality becomes popular, it will not be long until you will find robbers occupying your house on the pretext that they came to protect you from mythical robbers who might steal your watch next year.

D.D., 2–3

Thomism

It is only accidentally that St. Thomas belongs to the thirteenth century. His thought is no more confined to that period of human history than is the multiplication table.

G.I., xii

Thought (Modern)

There is no such thing as modernity in thought; there is only antiquity with new labels, like new advertisements. Modernity belongs only to the world of mechanics, but there is nothing new in the world of morals. From the fall of the angels up until the crack of doom there have been and will be only two moral systems possible: one is to live the way we think, the other is to think the way we live. The latter has always been called the "modern" and the other the "ancient" or "ancestral," but the modernity is only a matter of new tags and new labels and not one of new enthusiasms.

O.E., 173

Time

Time cannot be a savior, for time does not necessarily make things better; it often makes them worse.

M.P., 278

The more we notice Time, the less we are being interested.

M.T., 230

Each moment wasted means that life's precious treasures are diminished while the price for them becomes higher. Opportunities both rise in price and grow fewer every time we refuse to make use of them.

O.B., 26

Tolerance

A person is the most precious thing in the universe. A person is made in the image and likeness of God: every person bears within himself the Divine resemblance. The state exists for the person, and not the person for the state. No Irishman is to be tolerated! No Jew is to be tolerated! No American is to be tolerated! No German is to be tolerated! As persons, they are all *to be loved*. We have misunderstood tolerance when we say that one must be tolerant to certain persons.

L.I, 162

Tolerance and intolerance apply to two totally different things. Tolerance applies only to persons, but never to principles; intolerance applies only to principles but never to persons. We must be absolutely intolerant about the truths of mathematics, but we must be tolerant to the mathematician. We must not be broad-minded when we receive our bills and say that twenty and twenty *may* make sixty, but we must be tolerant to the grocer who makes the error. Nothing is so fearfully exclusive as truth. We must be intolerant about truth, for that is God's making and not ours. We must be tolerant to persons, for they are human and liable to error.

M.B., 200

Tolerance is an attitude of reasoned patience towards evil, and a forbearance that restrains us from showing anger or inflicting punishment. But what is more important than the definition is the field of its application. The important point here is this: Tolerance applies only to persons, but never to truth. Intolerance applies only to truth, but never to persons. Tolerance applies to the erring; intolerance to the error.

O.E., 103

. . . love of God and man, as an ideal, has lately been replaced by the new ideal of tolerance which inspires no sacrifices. Why should any human being in the world be merely tolerated? What man has ever made a sacrifice in the name of tolerance? It leads men, instead, to express their own egotism in a book or a lecture that patronizes the downtrodden group. One of the cruellest things that can happen to a human being is to be tolerated.

P.S., 176

Totalitarian Regimes

By their very nature they are anti-Christian because they exalt the herd recognized by the State, over the person whose value comes from God. That is why Totalitarianism persecutes the Church.

P.W., 31

Totalitarian Temptation

Despite all the pleas for liberty, it must be remembered that every flight from responsibility is a flight from liberty and every denial of personal guilt is also a denial of freedom. Cabbages cannot do wrong, though they have heads: adding machines cannot commit sins, though they do add and subtract. Perhaps it is the very burden of responsibility which flows from free choice that makes so many ready to surrender their great gift of freedom.

W.I., 68

Totalitarianism

Totalitarianism is wrong not because it has a dictator, but because the dictator dictates even to the soul of man by making the person a means to an end, man an economic aspect of the State, or a drop of blood in the body politic, or a worker in a State-factory.

F.G., 7

We live in an age where indifference to God and the moral law on the part of economics and politics, has led to an invasion of the soul by economics and politics. Such is the meaning of totalitarianism.

G.W., 61

Totalitarianism means the *total* possession of man: *body and soul*. A democracy leaves the soul free to serve its God. But totalitarianism cannot afford to allow the soul to be free. Hence it must persecute religion. Where the soul is, there is liberty. . . . To extinguish liberty, totalitarianism must persecute the soul. The exile of God always means the tyrannization of man.

L.I, 217

The basic principle of democracy is the sacredness of the individual as a creature endowed by God with inalienable rights. The basic principle of Nazism and other totalitarian systems is that the individual has no rights except those given him by the Party or the State. In America, freedom resides in man; in Nazism, freedom resides in the race. In America, man endows the State with rights which he received from God; in Nazism, the State endows man with rights which it got from Hitler.

P.W., 23

The Omnipotent State of Political Man has only one enemy, the Church. It knows it cannot absorb man totally, until it suppresses the Church which says that the soul belongs to God. That is why it persecutes the Church.

P.W., 114

Tradition

Tradition is the memory of society and without that tradition society cannot think.

O.E., 124

Nothing is more tragic in an individual who once was wise than to lose his memory, and nothing is more tragic to a civilization than the loss of its tradition.

P.S., 8

Tragedy

There can never be tragedy where men's conception of life is sordid. One of the essentials of tragedy is a belief in the dignity of human life. And a further condition of all tragedy is immortality. If there is no justice beyond the grave, then tragedy is pointless.

Because there is a God, because there is justice, because there is immortality, tragedy is something more than pain.

P.O., 331

Transcendence

A reasonable being should ask himself why—if chemicals can enter into plants, and plants be taken up into animals, and animals be taken into man—why man himself, who is the peak of visible creation, should be denied the privilege of being assimilated into higher power?

P.S., 234-235

The Trinity

Three in one, Father, Son, and Holy Ghost; three persons in one God; one in essence, distinction of persons, such is the mystery of the Trinity, such is the inner life of God.

D.R., 34

The Trivial

The souls of men are tried less by work than by the frustration that comes from too much attention to the trivial.

D.L., 30

Truth

Right is right if nobody is right, and wrong is wrong if everybody is wrong.

D.L., 139

It is easy to find Truth; it is hard to face it, and harder still to follow it.

L.H., 106

To want to speak the truth, it must be loved.

L.2, 67

Every religion in the world, I care not what it is, contains some reflection of one Eternal Truth. Every philosophy, every world-religion, every sect, contains an arc of the perfect round of the Natural and Revealed Truth. Confucianism has the fraction of fellowship; Indian asceticism has the fraction of self-abnegation; each human sect has an aspect of Christ's Truth.

P.R., 189

Truth never appeals to us unless it is personal. No purely philosophical system can long hold the devotion of men.

T.M., 83

The lover of truth is under an eternal law of rectitude; as he submits to it, he enjoys peace. Truth is not something that we invent; if we do, it is a lie; rather it is something we discover, like love.

W.I., 121

Truth is a narrow path; either side is an abyss. It is easy to fall either to the right or to the left; it was easy to be an idealist in the nineteenth century, as it is easy to be a materialist in the twentieth century; but to avoid both abysses and walk that narrow path of truth is as thrilling as a romance.

W.I., 122

Truth and Modern Philosophy

In philosophy, it contended that there was no such thing as Truth "with a capital T"; truth is purely ambulatory—we make it as we go. Truth is merely a point of view for each man is his own measure of what is true and what is good. Naturally, such a system produces as many philosophies as there are heads.

F.G., 13

Twentieth Century

. . . it is still true that the twentieth century is closer to God than the nineteenth century was. We are living on the eve of one of the great spiritual revivals of human history. Souls are sometimes closest to God when they feel themselves farthest away from Him, at the point of despair.

O.B., 86

The world had hoped for peace, and it got wars and rumors of wars; it was promised prosperity, and got starvation in the midst of plenty; it had hoped to make the world safe for democracy, and got a democracy which was hardly safe for the world; it was promised a world free from authority and got tyrannical dictatorship. The result is that today instead of Progress, Evolution, Prosperity, and World Peace, we have decay, unrest, uncertainty, doubt, and above all else a feeling of not knowing where we are going.

P.W., 18

Tyranny

We are just waking up to the old historical truth that the loss of God is the beginning of tyranny.

W.W., I I

U

Unbelief

Judas was more zealous in the cause of the enemy than he was in the cause of Our Lord. Men who leave the Church in like manner seek to atone for their uneasy consciences by attacking the Church. Since their consciences will not leave them alone, they will not leave the Guide of their consciences alone. The Voltaire who left the Church was the Voltaire who scoffed. Their hatred is not due to their unbelief, but their unbelief is due to their hatred. The Church makes them uneasy in their sin and they feel that if they could drive the Church from the world they could sin with impunity.

C.P., 22–23

There are two kinds of unbelief: those who say something is not true *because* they *wish* it were not true and those who say something is not true because they wish that it was. This latter kind is curable.

E.I., 73

The Unbeliever and War

Why out of an unspiritual universe should spiritual lives emerge? If there is no Beauty behind the universe, whence the Rose; if there is no Justice behind the universe, then whence comes our war for justice; if there is no distinction between good and evil, then how can our enemies be evil?

The unbeliever is confronted with more baffling difficulties by a war than the believer, for he cannot explain why all those things which should have brought happiness, brought disaster.

G.W., 6

Unhappiness

Two major causes of mental unhappiness are a want of purpose in life and an unrequited sense of guilt.

P.N., 143

United Nations

The United Nations never seems to see the inconsistency of the Soviets stirring up trouble through Africa and Asia and South America by inciting nationalism, while at the same time denying it to Poland and the other countries behind the Iron Curtain.

O.B., 288

United States

The United States has been an arsenal of defense against aggression; a Samaritan helping nations to rehabilitate themselves in peace; a pantry to the hungry and starving world; and, under Providence, the secondary cause for the preservation of the liberties of the free peoples of the world.

G.T., 145

Unity

Communism is not unity; it is compactness through fear, mobilization through arms, nationalization through propaganda, but it is not unity. Remove that fear, those armies, or that propaganda, and these nations would break up into thousands of discordant and warring elements. Only the spiritual is the basis of unity.

C., 95

The Universe

It is much easier to dwarf a little thing like man than to dwarf a big thing like the universe. . . . The imagery of the heavens as being two thousand million light-years in diameter is awesome when compared to the tiny earth, but trivial when compared to the imagery of the "hand that measured the heavens."

O.E., 20

University

When will some educators give us back a university?

D.L., 141

Some day under the pressure of catastrophe we will come to see that as science reveals nature, so theology reveals man. In that day, universities will be universities.

P.W., 78

University (Modern)

A multi-versity is made up of disparate and unconnected fields of
knowledge, in which one branch of knowledge seems to have no
relation with another body of knowledge; in which specialization
reaches a point where the department of biochemistry disagrees
with the department of biology, and both are in disagreement with
the department of genetics.

D.L., 139

The capacity for wonder is killed in many universities. Men emerge
interested in the question of whether they are at the top of the
class, or the foot, or somewhere in the middle, working their way
higher. This interest in the self and its rating poisons the proud
man's life—for self-centeredness is always a form of pride.

W.I., 100

The Unloved

Never a good word can be said for anyone. Because one is unloved
one tries to make everyone else unlovable. Characters are assassi-
nated, the noblest motives reduced to the basest, and slanders believed and propagated. When others do show them kindness they
look "for the catch in it"; even gifts are viewed with suspicion and
the sincerest of compliments acknowledged with a charge of insin-
cerity. Because such egotists are so miserable they seek to make
everyone else miserable. Never once do they see that they are the
cause of their own unhappiness. Someone else is always to blame.

W.H., 69

The Unredeemed

Perhaps if we understood human nature better, we would see that those who hate goodness and decency violently are also those who hate themselves more.

W.I., 64

Utilitarianism

How many Americans have a right to protest against Germany and Russia making utility the standard of right and wrong? Do we realize that the basic philosophy underlying much of American education for the last fifty years has been the philosophy of utility?

W.W., 25

If we look at the moral principles involved in the repudiation of treaties by Russia and Germany we see, if we are honest enough to admit it, the exaltation of American Pragmatism into a political philosophy. All that Hitler and Stalin did was to socialize our Pragmatism, substitute race utility and class utility for individual utility. If we are scandalized at seeing the truth give way to utility when worked out in Poland, why are we not so scandalized at seeing it worked out in the souls of our youth?

W.W., 26

V

Vacation

Rest never seems to be where we are, but other-where. Then when we get there, it seems to have gone somewhere else.

D.L., 47

A priest who would say: "I am on vacation, so I don't read Mass" has already confused vocation with vacation.

M.P., 167

The Vatican

Somewhere in this world is a sovereign State, though in territory it occupies only a few city blocks, one hundred and eight acres to be exact; it has no army, no guns, no defenses. One hundred armed men could capture it tomorrow morning if they wished. It has no selfish material interests anywhere on the face of God's earth. It wants only a space large enough for a crib on Christmas and for a cross on Good Friday to enlighten shepherds and wise men and draw all men to its refreshing redemption. . . . In the head of that sovereign state is the only hope of world peace—the *only hope*.

W.W., 81–82

Vatican II (Post)

In the Church began a yearning for the lusts of the world. Think of it! "In Egypt we had fish for the asking, cucumbers and melons, leeks and onions and garlic." Abortion, violence, divorce and repudiation of vows which belonged to the Egypt of the world were now by some accepted or defended. No longer was a solid, moral phalanx thrown up against the spirit of evil. It was no longer what the Church believed or the Holy Father taught, or what the Word of God cautioned; the individual conscience of and by itself became the sole standard of right and wrong: "Each of us doing what he pleases" (Deuteronomy 12:8).

M.P., 136

Vice

It will generally be found that all who are given to some so-called compulsive vice will generally seek out the companionship of those who will never blame them, but rather excuse them; that is, a kind of a confraternity of "innocent babes" is formed by which they insulate themselves from any "moral corruption."

G.T., 17

Victimhood

Victimhood means rather, a deep consciousness that we feel the guilt and sin of the world as if it were our own, and by constant union with Christ, seek to reconcile all mankind to Him. Love means identification with others—not only with the sheep in the sheepfold, but also those who are not in it. Many popularizers of Dietrich Bonhoeffer glorified his "wordly religion" without knowing that he defined it as identification of the priest-servanthood of Christ.

M.P., 32

Victory

A victory may be celebrated only on those fields in which a battle may be lost. Hence, in the divine order of things, God made a world in which man and woman would rise to moral heights, not by that blind driving power which makes the sun rise each morning, but rather by the exercise of that freedom in which one may fight the good fight and enjoy the spoils of victory, for no one shall be crowned unless he has struggled.

D.R., 44

Violence

The great difference between Communist and Christian violence is that Communist violence is directed against the neighbor, and Christian violence is directed against oneself. The Communist sword points outward to fellow man, the Christian sword points inward to egotism, to selfishness and to acquisitiveness, to lust and the thousand and one things which would make for antisocial elements in society. History supports the Christian position for never has it been known that violence and tyranny have of themselves realized liberty, or that strife achieved fraternity.

C.C., 91

The weapon to which the morally condemned reach is often violence. Nothing so much excites violence in a person or in a city as a bad conscience or a group of bad consciences.

M.P., 264

Violence in the past ended either with the attainment of a purpose, with exhaustion, or with a return to the past. But today, since violence is secondary to an ideology, it never ends. It is used to maintain a new aristocracy in power—not the aristocracy of blood, or ideas, or wealth, but the new élite of power. This new aristocracy does not care what cause it promotes as long as it can maintain its privileged position.

P.O., 90

Virtue

. . . many men sneer at virtue—because it makes vice uncomfortable.

L.C., 349

Vocations

When public relations techniques are used to promote vocations, with advertising in religious publications and direct mailings designed to encourage young people to join a given society or community, the danger is always present that stress will be placed on numbers to the neglect of quality. St. Thomas insists that the weeding out of the unfit is an obligation of those charged with the selection of candidates.

P.N., 81

Vow

The great advantage of the vow, which binds until death, is that it guards the couple against allowing the moods of time to override reason, and thus protects the general interests from canceling the particular. There is no other way to control capricious solicitation except by a vow. It may be hard to keep, but it is worth keeping because of what it does to exalt the characters of those who make it.

T.M., 180

W

War

No material profit, no conquest of any land, no crushing of any particular barbarities, can justify . . . crimson rivers, unless they purchase for us the greatest intangibles and imponderables of all: justice, peace and freedom.

S.P., III

Wars are not made by politics, but by politicians.

W.H., 167

War may be either a crusade or a curse: either a token of man's love of God, or the fruit of man's godlessness; either a sign that men are with God, or a token that they are *against* Him.

W.W., 1–2

Wealth

Credit-wealth, stocks, bonds, bank-balances, have no set limit at which we say, "No more." They have in them a caricature infinity, which allows men to use them as false religions, as substitutes for the true Infinity of God.

O.B., 96

When a man loves wealth inordinately, he and it grow together like a tree pushing itself in growth through the crevices of a rock. Death to such a man is a painful wrench, because of his close identification with the material. He has everything to live for, nothing to die for. He becomes at death the most destitute and despoiled beggar in the universe, for he has nothing he can take with him. He discovers too late that he did not belong to himself, but to things, for wealth is a pitiless master.

V.V., 97

Weariness

There are various kinds of weariness: weariness of the body, which can be satisfied under any tree or even on a pillow of stone; weariness of the brain, which needs the incubation of rest for new thought to be born; but hardest of all to satisfy is weariness of heart, which can be healed only by communion with God.

O.B., 61

Much of the weariness of the spiritual life is due to the constant necessity of bearing the shortcomings of others, along with the never ending strife against our own base inclinations.

W.I., 91

Weather

One wonders . . . as regards weather—if the modern man does not grumble far more about the weather than did his grandfather. He is able to make comparison with other climates because of his travels. But the older generation, which never had a suntan in January, was more satisfied with each day's weather as it came. As the Irish say when it is raining, "It is a good day to save your soul."

O.B., 89

Western Civilization

Western civilization with its Christian roots is not perishing; it is beginning to come into its own. The spread of democracy throughout the world, the formation of new nations rooted in the respect for human persons, the embarrassment of Communist dictatorships at their failure to give free suffrage to their people—all these represent the leavening process of the cult of the value of the individual.

F.D., 146

Will

There is only one thing in the world that is definitely and absolutely your own, and that is your will. Health, power, possessions and honor can all be snatched from you, but your will is irrevocably your own, even in hell. Hence, nothing really matters in life, except what you do with your will.

S.W., 25

We often delude ourselves into imagining that we have willed to be better, when we have made actually many reservations, have determined there are many present practices we will not change; then the willing is merely an idle wish. The key to spiritual advancement is to be found in the Creed: *"He descended into hell; the third day He arose again."*

W.H., 185

Wisdom

There are . . . two kinds of wisdom: wisdom of the flesh and the wisdom which God gives. One is very often opposed to the other. The first would say this is the only life there is; therefore, we should get all we can out of it. The other sees that this life is a kind of scaffolding up through which we climb to eternal happiness; it will, therefore, be so used as a ladder to the Mansions of the Heavenly Father. But this Divine Wisdom comes only to those who have qualifications for receiving it, and, as was pointed out above, one of the first conditions is good behavior. As Our Blessed Lord said, "If any man will do My Will, he will know My doctrine."

G.T., 64

Have not the great geniuses of all times confessed that after years of study they were still ignorant of truth, and that they seemed to stand merely on the shore of truth with its infinite expanse stretching before them? How often too, study in old age corrects the prejudices of youth, and how often those who have come to mock have remained to pray.

R.G., 328

Woman

A woman in professional life is happy when she has an occasion to be feminine.

L.2, 174

A woman is capable of more sacrifices than a man. Man is more apt to be a hero, through some great passionate outburst of heroism. But a woman's love makes a thousand small sacrifices, sprinkling them through the days and the months; their very repetition gives them the character of the commonplace. Not only her soul, but her body, has some share in the Calvary of Redemption; furthermore, she comes closer to death than man, whenever she brings forth a child.

L.5, 122

A woman . . . is much more a creature of time than man, and her security becomes less and less through the years. She is always much more concerned about her age than a man, and thinks more of marriage in terms of time. This is because a man is afraid of dying before he has lived, but a woman is basically afraid of dying before she has begotten life.

W.H., 66

The very emergence of woman into the political, economic, and social life of the world suggests that the world needs a continuity which she alone can supply; for while man is more closely related to things, she is the protector and defender of life. She cannot look at a limping dog, a flower overhanging a vase, without her heart and mind and soul going out to it, as if to bear witness that she has been appointed by God as the very guardian and custodian of life. Although contemporary literature associates her with frivolity and allurement, her instincts find repose only in the preservation of vitality. Her very body commits her to the drama of existence and links her in some way with the rhythm of the cosmos. In her arms, life takes its first breath, and in her arms, life wants to die. The word most often used by soldiers dying on the battlefields is "Mother." The woman with her children is "at home," and man is "at home" with her.

W.L., 130

Woman (Dignity of)

A civilization which no longer stands before God in reverence and responsibility has also renounced and denounced the dignity of woman, and the woman who submits and shares in such a divorce of responsibility from love stands in such a civilization either as a mirage or a pillar of salt.

W.L., 106–107

Womanhood

To the honor of womanhood it must forever be said: A woman was closest to the Cross on Good Friday, and first at the tomb on Easter Morn.

L.C., 407

The Word

It is that Word which St. John heard in the beginning of his Gospel, when he wrote: "In the beginning was the Word: and the Word was with God; and the Word was God."

Just as my interior thoughts are not made manifest without a word, so the Word in the language of John, "became flesh and dwelt amongst us."

And that Word is no other than the Second Person of the Blessed Trinity, the Word Who embraces the beginning and end of all things; the Word Who existed before creation; the Word Who presided at creation as the King of the Universe, the Word made flesh at Bethlehem, the Word made flesh on the Cross, and the Word made flesh dwelling in His divinity and humanity in the Eucharistic Emmanuel.

The Good Friday of twenty centuries ago did not mark the end of Him, as it did not mark the beginning. It is one of the moments of the Eternal Word of God.

L.A., 18–19

Words

What would be the general effect on the Nation if newspapers changed their vocabulary and began using old-fashioned words to express some unvarying and eternal truths? The question is pertinent because today words are so often used out of context that it is sometimes believed there is no reality behind them. . . . The Communists have had much to do with this since they began using the word "democracy" to describe their "tyranny," and "peace" for "war" through Fifth columnists, and "liberation" for "occupation."

D.L., 137

A kind word gives encouragement to the despondent heart, and a cruel word makes others sob their way to the grave.

W.I., 130

Work

The man who chooses his work because it fulfills a purpose he approves is the only one who grows in stature by working. He alone can properly say, at the end of it, "It is finished!"

W.H., 53

"To work is to pray." The well-regulated life does not defer prayer until work has been accomplished; it turns the work itself into a prayer. We accomplish this when we turn to God at the beginning and completion of each task and mentally offer it up for love of Him.

W.H., 53–54

We cannot get a real satisfaction out of our work unless we pause, frequently, to ask ourselves why we are doing it, and whether its purpose is one our minds wholeheartedly approve.

W.H., 56

Worker

. . . for the worker, there is little to choose between living at the sufferance of a Capitalist or living at the sufferance of a Party leader, for in either case, so long as he lives *by the will* of another he is not free.

S.P., 54

Workers and Communism

The Communist State, instead of protecting the workers against exploitation, rather protects the State through the exploitation of workers.

F.G., 97

Works

The test today is whether the Church will be identified with any culture. One thing is certain, if the Church marries the spirit of the age, she will be a widow in the next one. Those who are seeking to make the Church *wholly* an institution of "good works and social service" need but to recall that in the Letters to the Seven Churches in Revelation, Christ says: "I know your works." Works are important, but they cannot save souls, nor deliver us from the wrath of God.

M.P., 139

World

The world will allow only the mediocre to live. It hates the very wicked, like the thieves, because they disturb its possessions and security; it also hates the Divinely Good, because He disturbs its conscience, its heart and its evil desires.

M.P., 303

An almost forgotten truth, even among some practicing Christians, is that it is never the physical world, but only the spirit of the world that is evil; therefore the soul must detach itself from the world. "Love not the world, nor the things which are in the world. If any man love the world, the charity of the Father is not in Him" (I John 2:15).

P.S., 168–169

World (History of the)

. . . let it be recalled that never before in the history of the world has there been so much power and never before have men been so prepared to use that power for the destruction of human life; never before has there been so much gold, and never before has there been so much poverty; never before has there been so much wealth, and never before has there been such an economic crisis; never before has there been so much food, and never before has there been so much starvation; never before have there been so many facts and never before have there been so many unsolved problems; never before has there been so much education, and never before has there been so little coming to the knowledge of truth.

P., 38

World (Modern)

Modern politics, from monopolistic capitalism through socialism to communism, is the destruction of the image of man. Capitalism made a man a "hand" whose business it was to produce wealth for the employer; communism made man a "tool" without a soul, without freedom, without rights, whose task it was to make money for the State. Communism, from an economic point of view, is rotted capitalism. Freudianism reduced the Divine image of man to a sex organ which explained his mental processes, his taboos, his religion, his God, and his super-ego. Modern education denied, first, that he had a soul, then that he had a mind and finally that he had a consciousness.

M.P., 320

World War II

We want not victory alone—we had that in 1918; we want not merely the defeat of Germany and its Fuehrer—we had that in 1918; we want not a revengeful treaty of peace—we had that in 1918 we want not merely to make the world safe for democracy— we had that in 1918; we want not simply the crushing of barbarism —we had that in 1918.

This time we want something that was left out of Victory, left out of Versailles; left out of the so called peace, namely, the restoration to the world of a Justice based on the morality of God.

G.W., 11

This war is not a conflict of systems of politics, though a few superficial minds still think it is; it is a titanic struggle to decide whether the moral law of God shall be the basis of individual and social life, or the physical law of the ruthless sword.

G.W., 75

This war has knocked into a cocked hat all those vaporous theorizings of naturalist education which separated education from morality, which understood freedom of speech as freedom from morality; freedom of religion as freedom from worship; freedom from Fascism as freedom for Communism; freedom from fear as freedom from law; and freedom of thought as free.

S.P., 84

X Y Z

Yalta

Stalin lived up to the words he had spoken before Yalta: "Words have no relation to actions—otherwise what kind of diplomacy is it? Words are one thing; actions another. Good words are a mask for a concealment of bad deeds. Sincere diplomacy is no more possible than dry water or wooden air."

O.B., 276

Youth

Modern youth has little knowledge of two world wars, knows nothing of the Depression, and rather despises history as bunk. Convention is looked upon as a kind of restraint, a restriction, a manacle, a straitjacket; the culture which formed them is rejected; hence the fondness for placards, protests, adding signature to signature against anything which presently exists, whether it be religion, government, schools.

F.D., 11–12

The young are full of hopes for life is full of promise.

L.A., 52

Youth is too often judged by the few who express its worst side; crime makes better news than virtue.

L.4, 165

Youth today has a potential for sacrifice that has not been tapped. The appeal of Nazism, Fascism, and Communism was to youth and on the basis of dedication, consecration, and sacrifice to a race, a state, or a party. It would almost seem as if dictators had snatched the crucifix from our hands, torn the Christ from it, held it aloft, and said to youth: "Take up your cross daily and follow the dictator." Too often, we have, on the contrary, taken the Christ without His cross, a Redeemer without His means of Redemption, a Teacher to be equated with Buddha, Confucius, Tao.

M.W., 145

. . . how wrong George Bernard Shaw was when he said that it is a pity that youth has been wasted on the young. . . . The Good Lord knew it was better to put the illusions of life at the beginning in order that we might better discover the purpose of living as we grow closer to eternity.

O.B., 188

The youth of America remain juvenile longer than in any other country of the world! The reason is, that so-called "progressive" education by neglecting self-discipline in favor of unbounded self-expression has denied them the one thing that would make them really progressive.

S.W., 84

Every youth falls in love with the image of the possible, that is, with his dream walking, his emptiness filled, and his yearnings realized.

W.H., 103

Youth (Alienated)

The first stage is one of indifference: the son drifts away from his father and ignores his teachings, which he regards as undue restraints upon his freedom to do whatever pleases him. "The old man is behind the times," is his slogan at this period.

In the second stage, as the son intensifies the immorality of his living, indifference changes into hatred. He no longer thinks of his father *as* a father, but discounts his very humanity, saying, "The old man is a crack-pot." In the third stage, this hatred of his father expands to become hatred of the whole world, and the rebellious young man complains, "Nobody understands me."

W.H., 159

Youth (Cult of)

. . . the elders talk about "the future which is in the hands of the young"; everyone is afraid to speak of his age, and the subject of growing old is treated in a manner midway between an insult and a sneer.

P.S., 141

Youth versus Middle Age

Youth presses forward because of what will be; middle age becomes lost in the drabness of what is. Reality confronts middle age without the mask which it wore in youth. One is no longer sitting in the theater watching a romance; in middle age, one is taken behind the scenes and allowed to see the shabbiness of the costumes, the tinsel instead of the gold, and the painted forests.

O.B., 192

Yuppies

Transactions of business speculations in stocks, the ephemeral happenings of the day, the superficial wisdom of commentators—all these find a way directly to their hearts. But religion to them is weariness, when it is not humorous. Religion they say makes them melancholy and they want to relax.

S.C., 85

It is not particularly difficult to find thousands who will spend two or three hours a day in exercising, but if you ask them to bend their knees to God in five minutes of prayer they protest that it is too long.

V.V., 58

If there is any indication of the present degeneration of society better than another, it is the excess of luxury in the modern world. When men begin to forget their souls, they begin to take great care of their bodies. There are more athletic clubs in the modern world than there are spiritual retreat houses; and who shall count the millions spent in beauty shops to glorify faces that will one day be the prey of worms.

V.V., 58

Zacchaeus

One cannot imagine the Director of the Tax Bureau of any great city climbing a tree to see a parade, or to catch a glimpse of a visitor, but apparently Zacchaeus was more humble. When a man begins looking for God, he will soon discover that God is looking for him.

D.L., 90–91

Zeitgeist

To think clearly, one must remember that to marry the spirit of an age is to become a widow in the next one.

L.4, 18

Zoophilists

Medicine uses a high sounding and technical name for those who neglect their own families but gush over animals—zoophilists. Rousseau certainly was one; he abandoned his children, but had, we are told, a deep affection for his dog.

P.O., 34

Fulton Sheen Remembered

One of the outstanding memories I have of him is when I was on a train and had a compartment on my way to New York on the Southern Railroad. When a knock came at the door of the compartment, I was so tired; I was already stretched out and decided not to answer because I had several people already who wanted to speak to me. But the knock persisted. I opened the door, and there stood Bishop Fulton Sheen. I was amazed and honored. He came in, and we talked for nearly two hours. We talked about his ministry and mine and how different they were and yet how parallel they were.

On another occasion he was giving one of the last addresses that he ever gave at the National Prayer Breakfast. President Carter was the President at the time. I was asked by the committee if I would be ready to stand by in case Bishop Sheen could not carry on. He had his cardiologist with him. He looked very weak and tired and wan. However, when he stood up, the power of the Lord came upon him as I have seldom seen it come upon any man. He spoke with such conviction and authority—even turning to President and Mrs. Carter and stating in effect, "You both are sinners and need redemption." This was one of the straightest evangelical messages I have ever heard given at one of the National Prayer Breakfasts. His eyes flashed, and he was the old Fulton Sheen that we had known so long on television.

Our paths crossed on several other occasions at dinners or receptions or conferences where we both were speakers. I have the fondest recollections of him. I think he and I were the first on national television, in 1951. I remember watching him time after time and learning from him how to communicate to a television audience. He was a teacher and I was an evangelist. But in one sense we were both teachers and both evangelists with somewhat different gifts. He was a man of God and a man of prayer. I remember he was one of the first Catholic bishops I ever had a time of prayer with.

BILLY GRAHAM
December 30, 1988

Bishop Sheen was underrated as a thinker. I remember him particularly for one remark he made to me which was almost a prophecy. "Christendom is over," he said, "but not Christ." He was very ill when we met, and he died shortly afterwards; but his observation remains with me.

MALCOLM MUGGERIDGE
November 19, 1988

His pen produced over sixty books, as well as articles and letters that will never be numbered. Always he addressed himself to the thought of the times and insisted that a speaker must begin his message from where his hearers are, not where he is. . . . Many came to faith in Christ and the Church through his words, and for every famous name he instructed, there were hundreds of others who were just as important to him as those in the public eye. . . . We are all better off because he was in our midst and was our friend.

Archbishop EDWARD T. O'MEARA
from the Eulogy, December 13, 1979

In our lifetime we will not forget Fulton Sheen. His words will be forever; his messages touch the mind and the heart. Few men have that quality. Only love can supply that.

PEARL BAILEY
December 21, 1988

Bibliography of Fulton J. Sheen Works Cited with Abbreviations

A.   *Treasure in Clay: The Autobiography of Fulton J. Sheen.* Garden City, N.Y.: Doubleday, 1980.

C.B.   *The Cross and the Beatitudes.* New York: P. J. Kenedy and Sons, 1937.

C.   *The Cross and the Crisis.* Milwaukee: Bruce Publishing Co., 1938.

C.C.   *Communism and the Conscience of the West.* New York: Bobbs-Merrill, 1948.

C.I.   *Rejoice* (formerly *Christmas Inspirations*). Garden City, N.Y.: Doubleday, 1984.

C.M.   *Calvary and the Mass.* New York: P. J. Kenedy and Sons, 1936.

C.P.   *Characters of the Passion.* New York: P. J. Kenedy and Sons, 1946.

D.D.   *A Declaration of Dependence.* Milwaukee: Bruce Publishing Co., 1941.

D.L.   *Thoughts for Daily Living.* Garden City, N.Y.: Garden City, 1955.

D.R.   *The Divine Romance.* New York: Century Co., 1930.

D.V.   *The Divine Verdict.* New York: P. J. Kenedy and Sons, 1943.

E.G.   *The Eternal Galilean.* New York: Appleton-Century-Crofts, 1936.

E.I.   *Crossways* (formerly *Easter Inspirations*). Garden City, N.Y.: Doubleday, 1984.

F.D.   *Footprints in a Darkened Forest.* New York: Meredith Press, 1967.

F.G.   *Freedom Under God.* Milwaukee: Bruce Publishing Co., 1940.

G.C.   *For God and Country.* New York: P. J. Kenedy and Sons, 1941.

G.I.   *God and Intelligence.* New York: Longmans, 1949.

G.T.   *Guide to Contentment.* Garden City, N.Y.: Doubleday, 1970.

G.W.   *God and War.* New York: P. J. Kenedy and Sons, 1942.

H.C.   *The Hymn of the Conquered.* Indiana: Our Sunday Visitor, 1933.

J.S.   *Jesus, Son of Mary.* New York: Declan X. McMullen, 1947.

L.A.   *Love One Another.* New York: P. J. Kenedy and Sons, 1944.

L.C.   *Life of Christ.* Garden City, N.Y.: Doubleday, 1977.

L.E.   *Liberty, Equality and Fraternity.* New York: Macmillan, 1938.

L.H.   *Lift Up Your Heart.* Garden City, N.Y.: Garden City, 1942.

L.L.   *The Life of All Living.* Garden City, N.Y.: Doubleday, 1979.

L.1   *Life Is Worth Living.* New York: McGraw-Hill, 1953.

L.2   *Life Is Worth Living* (Second Series). New York: McGraw-Hill, 1954.

L.4   *Life Is Worth Living* (Fourth Series). New York: McGraw-Hill, 1956.

L.5   *Life Is Worth Living* (Fifth Series). New York: McGraw-Hill, 1957.

M.B.   *The Mystical Body of Christ.* New York: Sheed and Ward, 1935.

M.P.   *Those Mysterious Priests.* Garden City, N.Y.: Doubleday, 1974.

M.T.   *Moods and Truths.* Garden City, N.Y.: Garden City, 1950.

M.U.   *The Moral Universe.* Milwaukee: Bruce Publishing Co., 1936.

M.W.   *Missions and the World Crisis.* Milwaukee: Bruce Publishing Co., 1963.

O.B.   *On Being Human.* Garden City, N.Y.: Doubleday, 1982.

O.E.   *Old Errors and New Labels.* Garden City, N.Y.: Garden City, 1950.

P.   *The Prodigal World.* Indiana: National Council of Catholic Men, 1936.

PH.   *Philosophy of Science.* Milwaukee: Bruce Publishing Co., 1934.

P.N.   *The Priest Is Not His Own.* New York: McGraw-Hill, 1963.

P.O.   *Philosophy of Religion.* New York: Appleton-Century-Crofts, 1948.

P.R.   *Preface to Religion.* New York: P. J. Kenedy and Sons, 1946.

P.S.   *Peace of Soul.* Garden City, N.Y.: Doubleday, 1954.

P.W.   *Philosophies at War.* New York: Scribner's, 1943.

R.G.   *Religion Without God.* New York: Longmans, 1928.

R.S.   *The Rainbow of Sorrow.* New York: P. J. Kenedy and Sons, 1938.

S.C.   *Seven Words to the Cross.* New York: P. J. Kenedy and Sons, 1944.

S.L.   *The Seven Last Words.* New York: Appleton-Century Co., 1935.

S.P.   *Seven Pillars of Peace.* New York: Scribner's, 1944.

S.V.   *The Seven Virtues.* Garden City, N.Y.: Garden City, 1953.

S.W.   *Seven Words of Jesus and Mary.* Garden City, N.Y.: Garden City, 1953.

T.A.   *These Are the Sacraments.* New York: Hawthorn, 1962.

T.C.   *The True Meaning of Christmas.* London: Peter Davies, 1955.

T.M.   *Three to Get Married.* New York: Appleton-Century-Crofts, 1951.

T.T.   *Thinking Life Through.* New York: McGraw-Hill, 1955.

V.V.   *Victory over Vice.* New York: P. J. Kenedy and Sons, 1939.

W.I.   *Way to Inner Peace.* Garden City, N.Y.: Garden City, 1955.

W.H.   *Way to Happiness.* Garden City, N.Y.: Garden City, 1954.

W.L.   *The World's First Love.* Garden City, N.Y.: Doubleday, 1956.

W.W.   *Whence Come Wars.* New York: Sheed and Ward, 1940.

Fulton J. Sheen Works Not Cited in the Text

The Armor of God. New York: P. J. Kenedy and Sons, 1943.
Children and Parents. New York: Simon and Schuster, 1970.
Go to Heaven. New York: McGraw-Hill, 1960.
God Love You. Garden City, N.Y.: Garden City, 1955.
The Power of Love. New York: Simon and Schuster, 1965.
That Tremendous Love. New York: Harper and Row, 1967.
This Is Rome. New York: Hawthorn, 1960.
This Is the Holy Land. New York: Hawthorn, 1961.
This Is the Mass. New York: Hawthorn, 1958.
The Way of the Cross. New York: Appleton-Century-Crofts, Inc., 1932.

Index of Topics

This index includes only those topics in an excerpt other than the topic under which that excerpt is listed in the text.

ABOUT THE EDITORS

George J. Marlin, a specialist in municipal finance, is a vice president and senior portfolio manager at the United States Trust Company of New York. Mr. Marlin is also a general editor of *The Collected Works of G. K. Chesterton* and an editor of *The Quotable Chesterton* and *More Quotable Chesterton*. Mr. Marlin's articles have appeared in numerous periodicals, including *The Chesterton Review, Fidelity, The Daily Bond Buyer, Credit Markets, Muni-Markets,* and *The Wanderer.* Born in 1952, Mr. Marlin resides in New York City.

Richard P. Rabatin, a professional musician, resides in Stony Brook, New York. Born in 1950, Mr. Rabatin received his undergraduate degree from the State University of New York at Stony Brook. He received his masters degree at Fordham University in political science, and he studied musical composition at Berklee College of Music in Boston. Mr. Rabatin is also a general editor of *The Collected Works of G. K. Chesterton* and an editor of *The Quotable Chesterton* and *More Quotable Chesterton*. His articles have appeared in *The Chesterton Review* and *Fidelity.*

John L. Swan is a partner in the community relations firm Institutional Planning and Development Corporation. He was formerly associated with the National Broadcasting Corporation and the American Cancer Society. Mr. Swan, a lifelong resident of New York City, is also a general editor of *The Collected Works of G. K. Chesterton* and an editor of *The Quotable Chesterton* and *More Quotable Chesterton*.